THE
RULES OF
CHAOS

by Stephen Vizinczey

IN PRAISE OF OLDER WOMEN

THE
RULES OF
CHAOS

or, Why Tomorrow Doesn't Work

STEPHEN VIZINCZEY

The McCall Publishing Company

NEW YORK

Library of Congress Catalog Card Number: 75-107894

SBN 8415-0000-2

Design by Tere LoPrete

The McCall Publishing Company
230 Park Avenue, New York, N.Y. 10017

PRINTED IN THE UNITED STATES OF AMERICA

To Gloria

*"Nearly all our miseries in life
come from our false notions of
what is actually happening to us
. . . thus to judge events sanely
is a great step toward happiness"*
STENDHAL: *Journal*, 10 December 1801

THE
RULES OF
CHAOS

From London to Dover

HAVE YOU ever been in the emergency ward of a hospital? Patients who are conscious and able to talk are as upset about the *unexpectedness* of what happened to them as they are about their injuries.

One sunny morning I was driving with three friends from London to Dover when the car went off the A2 at seventy miles an hour, hit a patch of gravel, flew into the air, and turned upside down to crash on its canvas top. In the split second before certain death, I remember thinking: it's going to be quick. The car fell to pieces, but we escaped with slight injuries. For a few moments we were numb with joy, testing our unbroken limbs; yet half an hour later, in the emergency ward, I saw only sullen faces around me. We had all been so sure we'd be in Calais by lunchtime. We felt betrayed.

It is in such bitter moments, in the stunned surprise of twisting one's ankle, that one wonders how life works.

A Murder

"I'M A MURDERER on the prowl," the killer introduces himself, brandishing his knife.

"Obviously," sighs the Sophisticate. People keep telling him things he's already noticed, that's the curse of his life.

"This is a good carving knife," the man claims with pride.

"Yes, I can see that," agrees Sophisticate with a condescending nod. A knife is a knife, it looks like a knife, so why remark on it? Is he supposed to reflect upon anything as commonplace as a carving knife?

"It's a good, strong bit of steel," the killer says, eager for a little recognition, "it's real sharp, cuts meat with no trouble."

"Of course it does, that's quite true." Sophisticate nods again, with growing boredom. Sharp knives cut well, what of it, he cannot be bothered with truisms; and he yawns just before he is stabbed. His last moment is his first surprise.

The serenity of the stupid comes from confusing knowing with understanding.

The Game of Detection

YOU KNOW everything—all truths are self-evident. The trick is to keep them in mind, to relate them to each other, to gauge their significance.

This is the game I invite you to play, a game of reflection and detection, a test of your willingness to reconsider the most natural assumptions and of your ability to pick up clues, spot connections and make cross-references without prompting—you'll need some of the skills of Philip Marlowe, Hercule Poirot, and Chief Inspector Blaise Pascal. There are penalties of varying severity: for instance, the player who fails to notice the connection between the psychological plights of an ugly, poor, once-lucky lover and three successive Presidents of the United States shall lose a vital point of insight.

The winner gets the philosopher's cup.

Leda and the Swan by Ammannati, Bargello, Florence (BETTMANN ARCHIVE)

Rule Number One

THE FUTURE IS
A BLINDING MIRAGE

I

WHAT HAPPENS in the next moment is never as certain as it appears before or after.

Nothing follows as a matter of course, not even this sentence, not if you have a sudden toothache, or the book is uncomfortable to hold, or you think you'd rather read the paper after all, or if someone calls you and you must listen—if you're in bed we have a better chance to complete the sentence, you're trapped, but you may turn over and feel drowsy, there is someone beside you who wants to make love or can't sleep with the light on, there's a power failure, there's a fire!—so if we reach the end now, you must admit it was touch and go.

There are more possibilities in each situation than we could be bothered to think about, or would be able to imagine even if we bothered. It is impossible to predict with absolute assurance what will happen in the next second.

I I

ANYTHING MIGHT HAPPEN. But if this is so, why do we consider some events "logical" and others "accidental"? If one's car can go off the road just as easily as it can arrive at one's destination, then each event is an accident.

Whether we see an event as accidental or logical depends not on the event itself but on our expectations. Traffic experts consider X-number of road casualties the natural and indeed inevitable outcome of a Labor Day weekend, but to those involved they are tragic absurdities.

Mr. Bottom calculates in his office that, out of 25,000,-000 drivers on the road, between 210 and 220 will suffer fatal injuries, and then drives off to his fishing resort, a contented oracle. His family mourns him, reflecting how little the law of averages has to do with any single occurrence.

Good hunters the world over mistake each other for game, but at the start of the season it is impossible to foretell which lucky hunter will get the trophy and which will be carried home.

I I I

IN THE ANCIENT TOWN of Velletri, south of Rome, I have a friend who used to go hunting birds and rabbits in the Alban Hills, until he was shot in the groin. Except for Bruno's particular ill luck, the event was easily explained, its cause being perfectly straightforward: his assailant took him for a partridge.

There was a *reason* for everything that has ever happened; so in the past everything makes sense, everything appears logical.

Only when we consider an event in the light of other possibilities which did *not* materialize, when we think of some of the circumstances that could have produced quite contrary results, do we begin to sense how chancy the past was when it happened. How was it that the two of you met?

LET THE SQUARES RUN, for we are now going to improve on Newton. Without a degree in physics, by the authority of sheer impertinence. I feel myself back in school, I feel on me the disapproving eyes of the teacher, I'm a speck of ignorant dust—yes, it all started to go wrong in school.

We learned about absolute laws and inevitable processes, one by one, in isolation, and so we tend to assume that all those laws are going to work and all those processes are bound to run their course. But in reality they don't necessarily do so, for they don't operate in a vacuum as in a classroom demonstration (the universe is a crowded place) and they are constantly contending and interfering with each other.

Newton's apple may fall to the ground, but if there happens to be a gale, the force of the wind will overcome the force of gravity, and the apple will fly through the air and end up on the roof. Life is chaos not because there are no laws, but because there are innumerable laws and they are constantly in haphazard collision.

Apples fall to the ground or fly upward.

V

STILL, I DON'T claim that I'm floating in the air as I write this, nor am I advising you to step out of the window—the laws of nature do create certainties of a certain kind.

So let's pay restrained homage to determinism by contemplating a beautifully carved marble statue which came out of the tip of a paintbrush. Michelangelo painted *Leda and the Swan* on canvas, but the French (in one of their not all that infrequent fits of prudery) destroyed Michelangelo's work, and all that is left to us is Ammannati's marble copy—such unexpected transformations of substance are not uncommon in our chaotic world. Yet, the limitless possibilities of life and the artist's imagination notwithstanding, it is absolutely certain that no lady ever made love with a swan, even if beneath the beast's feathery exterior there throbbed the mighty heart of Greece's top god, famed for his resourcefulness. Michelangelo-Ammannati did not exaggerate: the swan evidently hasn't got anything big enough to disturb Leda's relaxed cool. But even so, the statue is one of the more stimulating demonstrations of the impossible.

As well as banning some kinds of intercourse, the laws of nature can always be counted on to manifest themselves, but rarely in direct progression (as they would if they worked in a vacuum or as they do when they don't happen to be interfered with). They manifest themselves not so much through action as through reaction.

Could I possibly trouble you, dear reader, for a glass of water with a couple of ice cubes in it, just to make sure it's really cold? I wanted to draw your attention—thank you—to the fact that it isn't the nature of water to steam away, it would never act so airily on its own, this is simply the way it *reacts* to 212° Fahrenheit heat. Now I hope that you'll put the water, the ice cubes and the steam together and will be jolted into the realization that even such an innocent thing as a slow-running river is capable of more tricks than the Academy of Science could dream of.

Is there a reader who doesn't think so? Well, if he can't be bothered to take nature's hints, if he has the mental laziness, the complacency to presume that he or any man can tell what water will do next, just because it is known to remove itself from a hot spot in an elusive manner—then I'm throwing his drink in his face, stuffing his ice cubes down his collar, hoping they'll freeze his spine. Then I'll boil him in water. He must be saved from his lack of imagination—right now he's so dumb he's positively dangerous to himself and his unlucky relations. A man who can't even put stream and steam together is unlikely to suspect that water can also turn into cancer in his stomach, if his friendly neighborhood industrialist and the experts at the Atomic Energy Commission keep putting poisonous waste into his pipelines. He'll die a horrible death, but I'll not mourn him—for he has never mourned the universe, never taken the trouble to perceive its sadness, and he won't be with us on the barricades to defend Mother Nature against the rapist labcoats—heavens, it's true, they *are* motherfuckers! To think of that poor, schizophrenic woman, already tormented by billions of conflicting habits, having to suffer the indignity of being fingered by her own sons, who positively enjoy adding to her chaotic misery!

. . . I'm sorry. Emotional outbursts are unseemly, but I found the possible presence of unimaginative idiots insufferable. Now that we're in more select company, I wish to apologize and promise to mind my manners. Where were we?

What we assume (regardless of our purely theoretical knowledge) about nature's behavior is what we have already experienced, what we have become accustomed to. What happened to come to pass in the past is what we take for granted in the future. In each of us there is a bit of

Michael Frayn's hero in *Against Entropy*, who could not understand how he could possibly be middle-aged when *he had been young all his life!* Thus it is difficult for most people to conceive that the air which gives them life with every breath can also poison them if it is polluted, or that the peaceful trout can turn into a man-killer if his river is passing by the latest death-factory. Once we are born, nature ensures that we shall grow up, unless something untoward happens to us; but we have a better chance to live (as I tried to explain to the wretched clod who has just left us) if we appreciate that not even the natural processes contained in our bodies and producing our feeling of contentment and security are free from interference and drastic alteration.

V I

THE DIFFERENCE between seeing the world as orderly or chaotic is the difference between seeing it as standing still or in motion. Theoretically it would be possible to figure out how any element or organism would react in any given situation, but the impassable barrier to foresight and order is that the situation is not given, it is yet to occur. Nature has billions of definable characteristics, just as you or I have a few, but our character is not our life history. Nature is not what is, but what occurs, through the haphazard interplay of events.

The tree has its own pattern of growth and so does the lightning. However, it is through their fortuitous conjunction in time and place that the particular tree is destroyed.

But I consulted nature only for a clue to our own affairs,

and on second thought I find I was wrong about Leda and the swan. The Greeks knew what they were about when they invented Zeus and spent a great deal of time celebrating his impossible exploits. It would be better for us to allow that the swan succeeded in his embrace and had a good time of it; we should rather think ill of Leda than underestimate the infinite possibilities of our destiny.

V I I

Scene: IRT, 5:27 P.M.

In the packed subway car, Harry Determinism is pushed against the ravishing backside of a girl wearing the shortest possible skirt. With all the shoving and twisting of rush hour the miniskirt slides up, and Harry cannot prevent himself from reaching out and under and squeezing the sweet little thing, who turns out to be a policewoman in the scantest disguise, looking for muggers. Harry D. tries to explain to the judge that the crime was the inevitable consequence of a particular law of nature—and indeed it looks even more inevitable if we consider how tightly pressed they were and how the pretty police sergeant was waiting for just such an unseemly pass. But if we consider all the immediate causes of the crime (including the sergeant's eagerness to detect one, Harry's bad morals and her good looks, the crowded subway, etc.), we must conclude that none of these was *decisive*, that they had created merely the possibility of what occurred. What turned the latent possibility into the actual squeezing, what brought all the dormant causes into play—and thus was the decisive cause

(*15*)

of the event—was the two persons' accidental meeting in a non-face-to-face position.

If only the policewoman had caught another bugger wet-handed a couple of minutes earlier, if only Mr. Determin-ism hadn't succeeded in pushing his way into the car just as the doors were closing, if only he had been swept behind the next girl, a tall, formidable blonde who might have acknowledged a gesture of indecent affection with an in-dulgent smile (which would have been a quite different sort of event—not that Harry would have dared) . . . Over a hundred pages could be written about the totally haphazard events of just the previous half hour which could have saved Harry from a bad scare, a stern lecture and a fine.

Once the two protagonists collided in a certain manner at a precise moment in a particular place, the event was the logical outcome of a great many "causes," from the law of Harry's nature to the mores of modern society and the insufficiency of public transport in our overpopulated cities; but the fact that he and she happened to be at the same spot in the same second was not logical at all. It could be explained only by the principle of chance.

The quick-thinking reader, good at making his own cross-references, will have already detected here a glimmer of Tolstoy's insight into history.

V I I I

IN REVIEWING historians' explanations for the outbreak of the French Revolution, the cranky genius was dissatisfied with all of them. He ridiculed those who attribute it to the vile royal governments of France or to the radical ideas of French writers. ("Certain people," Tolstoy parodies the ideological historian, "were at this time writing books. At the end of the eighteenth century there had gathered in Paris a couple of dozen persons who began talking about all men being equal and free. Because of this, over the length and breadth of France men fell to slaughtering and destroying one another. . . .") And indeed, even if we add up these and many other causes—the squandering of France's resources on Versailles and on military adventures, the exploitation of the land and the peasantry to maintain a fainéant aristocracy, unemployment in the cities, the wretchedness of the sansculottes, the restiveness of a merchant class with more money than power—all the sort of socio-economic-political developments which delight the trend-carrying experts of the White House—we still cannot answer Tolstoy's question why the revolution broke out in France when it did. ("How is it that Louis XIV and Ivan the Terrible live out their reigns in peace, while Louis XVI and Charles I are put to death by their peoples?")

Tolstoy observes that no "general" explanation of historical events can withstand the question why they occurred at that precise moment, and he concludes that the notion of cause does not apply to history.

I X

WHAT WE USUALLY think of as the causes of an event constitute merely the "scene," the general situation which excludes certain kinds of events but still allows for a great number of them, only one of which will actually occur.

What *does* occur depends not on the conditions (matters of years, decades, centuries, countries, continents) but on other events (matters of the immediate moment and place) which create the occasion.

Had Harry Determinism been a homosexual, he would never have committed that particular indecent assault, and in this sense his eager heterosexuality (his general condition for years, perhaps from birth) allowed for the possibility of his crime. But his actually committing it was the result of the moment's opportunity, created by other events occurring at that very time and place.

Every event, be it a subway incident or the storming of the Bastille, is the outcome of other events occurring at the same time and place but otherwise unconnected. How totally fortuitous is any combination of simultaneous occurrences can be seen from the fact that the addition or removal of one single occurrence (and this out of dozens or millions) would have totally changed the nature and effect of the combination. Had a courtier poisoned Marie Antoinette (as several intended to, for reasons having nothing to do with Rousseau or the hunger of Parisians), or had a heavy rain fallen in Paris on 14 July 1789, the storming of the Bastille might not, indeed almost certainly would not, have occurred. The delay of the revolution due to unfavorable weather conditions could have given the Marie Antoinette faction time to cancel the policy of halfhearted reforms in favor of a law-and-order bloodbath which might have lasted for quite a while. Of course the Bastille might still have been torn apart either sooner or later—but this is also to say that it might still be standing, a minor tourist attraction.

The convergence of otherwise unrelated events at a particular time and place (and the result of this combination) can only be described as a coincidence—the work of chance.

X

AT THIS point my wife stopped typing my manuscript and marched in to protest. "You're talking as though *everything* depended on chance. There's nothing accidental about the birth of a child!" Martha, who reads *Private Eye* and *The Realist* and knows about the darker side of life, cuts her mother short: "You mean after the baby's conceived, by some fluke, there's nothing to prevent its birth—except maybe a miscarriage?"

In truth, lovemaking and conception are as good an example as any of how the chance of the split second materializes opportunities or renders them stillborn.

X I

THE LONGER we reflect on the way things happen, the more we doubt the existence of an orderly world—so we don't reflect too much. Though nobody would deny the existence of chance, we all tend to think and act as if there were no such thing. We ignore, minimize, overlook its importance, if we don't forget about it altogether.

Ladies and gentlemen, I appeal to your pride in your intelligence! Let's give chance its due.

As CUSTOM DEMANDS that all important news should be delivered as grave news, and as I'm not dressed for a solemn occasion (I just realized that I don't even have my footnotes on), I must ask you to help out by contributing more than your usual share of seriousness, for what follows ought to affect most of your attitudes and ideas about life.

There is nothing erratic about time—moment follows moment, day after day. Similarly, there is nothing disorderly about space, at least within our world. It can be measured with old rulers—inch after inch, mile after mile—space is positively petrified. It is the combination of time and space that creates chaos: the momentary situation, the simultaneous presence of otherwise unrelated events at the time of a place, in the place of a time.

The convergence of otherwise unrelated events $=$
time $+$ *place* $=$ *chance*

The decisive cause of every event is pure chance.
Events do not develop, they are born out of chaos.

X I I I

"JUST THE SAME," my wife says, "days pass without any surprises."

I must think that over. It is impossible to examine any single event without discovering how decisive chance was in bringing it about—either by creating an unexpected turn or by allowing the expected to happen in unforeseen ways, either in the shape of an "accident" or a "narrow escape."

Yet we can't possibly bother pondering how it was that we succeeded in catching the bus we intended to take, and the infrequency of actual surprises has a great deal to do with how little we think of chance.

How could we grasp, then, that life is chaotic despite the infrequent emergence of chaos? that we are always subject to chance even when it does not manifest itself?

"We die only once," I tell her, "but we are mortal all the time."

X I V

ONE OF CHAPLIN's favorite and deepest jokes was the little man's obliviousness of the dangers all around him. He is having a quiet meal of his boiled shoes, up in the snowy mountains of Alaska, as his wooden shack slides slowly over a precipice. He gets up to fetch the salt from the other end of the room; the floor he is walking on is already over empty space, and with every step the shack tilts further to hurl him to certain death. But he finds the salt just in time to walk back to his table, restoring the precarious balance of the hut. His life was saved by the most extraordinary, not to say incredible, coincidence, but he salts his shoes as if everything was in order.

We all tend to be similarly unaware of chance's contribution to our survival and successful completion of our tasks. Unless the accidental nature of life manifests itself against our expectations in the most drastic manner, we are oblivious of it.

We need imagination to perceive what happens.

LETTER TO Mr. Neil Armstrong, first moon man:

Dear Mr. Armstrong:
I think it wasn't very gallant of you to forget to pay
tribute to Lady Luck, who was your attentive and
obliging bunny throughout your voyage. As you took
off, your boosting expert Von Braun complained publicly that people were not psychologically prepared for
something going wrong; but as nothing did, now everyone is pretending that there was no woman with you in
the capsule. She is being disowned like a common pros-
titute!
And what, pray, sir, will become of you and me, of
all of us, if she takes offence and moves to another
galaxy?

Sincerely yours,
A Concerned Citizen

X V I

"You're GETTING to be a bore about chance."
"Who's talking about chance? I'm talking about our
suicidal faith in the future and human power."
"Oh."

X V I I

IN SAN FRANCISCO a couple of years ago, I met a radio
reporter who was planning to get married.
"Thanks," he said diffidently when I wished him good

luck. He made an uncertain grimace. "I'll need it. You never can tell how it'll turn out, can you?" Although the marriage was to involve only himself and a girl he knew well, or at least thought he did, he couldn't help feeling apprehensive.

But he was dead certain about the future of Asia, which involved some two thousand million human beings and countless political situations fraught with more possibilities than the most farfetched marital farce. He had no doubt whatever that if America withdrew from Vietnam, "the whole of Asia would go communist."

X V I I I

OUR ABILITY to foresee and influence events diminishes with extension in time and space.

We cannot know what will happen in the next second, but we can make a reasonable guess; the next day is less certain, next week and next month are still more obscure, and what we think about next year is pure fantasy.

Similarly, any situation involving only oneself is far more predictable and controllable than situations which involve others as well. If you happen to be alone with this book in a hotel room in a strange city, late at night, your intention to read has a chance to dominate circumstances; but if you are at home with your family early in the evening, the effectiveness of your desire to read is sharply reduced.

What is curious about all this is that our confidence in foretelling and influencing events increases in inverse ratio to our ability to do so. We're more aware of what is close to us and thus we're also more aware of what may go wrong with our calculations. The farther we go from

(23)

ourselves and from the present, the less we sense the probabilities, and it is easy for us to be "dead certain" about things we cannot possibly know anything about.

We continually extend the logic of the momentary situation into the future, with little thought for the countless possibilities which materialize changes faster than we can blink. So politicians are forever compelled to announce "unforeseen developments" with the pathetic bravado of palm readers who are amazed to hear that the poor girl didn't meet the handsome millionaire they promised her. Then the new and surprising momentary situation is itself projected into the future, trapping us in yet another mirage.

Moreover, we misunderstand the present by looking at today through the haze of yesterday's expectations, and the misinterpretations accumulate. That is how we grow old and "out of touch" long before our senses fail us. Dr. Gallup remarked that the main thing he had learned from polltaking was that people were incapable of perceiving anything new after the age of forty.

Thus aging politicians are prepared to destroy the world in the name of such dead concepts as communism and free enterprise; the old fight the battles of the past in more ways than one. But wars are only the most sickening examples of the logic of blinding expectations. We are still obsessed with totalitarianism, for instance, because in the past industrialization extended the influence of central authority and we assumed that, as technology continued to expand, so would the power of the state. In fact, as technology has developed, it has become an agent of disruption by making smaller groups more self-sufficient and self-assertive and states more vulnerable than ever (the hijacking of airplanes is but one of the more obvious signs). Yet while technology is bringing political disintegration upon us, we are still trying to ward off the monolithic superstate of *Nineteen Eighty-Four*. Will 1984 be the year of independence for Scotland, Quebec, and New York City? California?

X I X

I MUST DISOWN my last questions. It is preposterous to suggest, however tentatively, that parts of Britain, Canada, and the United States will secede in the same decade, let alone in the same year or, indeed, necessarily ever. Such a proposition could be inspired only by the idiotic notion of chain reactions in history. But then we hear inanities so often that we fall back on them unawares, even if we have already seen through them in some of our brighter moments. This is why it is a strain to think at all: with so many falsehoods being drilled into us daily, we must continually struggle to regain lost ground, instead of getting farther ahead. Who can blame those who give up?

But at any rate, let's not give in to the idea that there is such a thing as a "chain reaction" in human affairs. History may yet be reduced to the logic of nuclear explosions, but it is still too early to equate man's chaotic destiny with the deadly simplicity of the Bomb. God knows, the great powers, incited by their learned experts, try hard enough to confuse the two.

Russia and the United States nearly blew up the earth over the chain reaction of revolutions which Cuba was supposed to ignite in Latin America, though there is still no sign of it after eleven years of Castroism. This, of course, didn't deter the United States from getting lost in the Vietnam jungle, just in case the Latin American revolution might take off from there. The Russian leaders, inheritors of another revolution that was supposed to sweep the world but didn't, were similarly undeterred from invading Czechoslovakia, delivering another blow to their crumbling satellite system and straining further the tolerance to their rule at home and abroad. And they did this, we're told, for a sound if unsporting reason—to prevent Czechoslovakia from setting off storms through the length and breadth of the Soviet empire.

The truth is, of course, that millions of otherwise unrelated circumstances and events must simultaneously occur to ignite a revolution, even in the most embittered country, and these cannot be *arranged* to coincide or be generated by the power of example. Indeed, if a revolution next door or the landing of a guerrilla party or any definable set of happenings could set off a great many people (all at once and just at the right moment) to risk their lives for the overthrow of their despised rulers, few governments would survive long enough to collect taxes. By the same token, if the "power of example," the extermination or the toleration of radicals, or any other calculable actions or events could be decisive in preventing revolutions, no dictator would lose a night's sleep.

Yet, despite such obvious considerations, governments can perpetrate horrors (with a great deal of popular approval) on the basis of their sincerely held but nonetheless brazen delusion that they know what would happen in the future of infinite possibilities, but for their intervention.

X X

WHAT SUPERNATURAL magic we attribute to human intentions can be seen from the inane argument concerning the maxim "the end justifies the means." Some say it does, some say it doesn't, but each side equates the hoped-for end with the end result—as if the aim of our activities had some direct relationship to their actual outcome—as if going to prison justified robbing a bank.

"The end justifies the means" is an utterly irrational statement assuring us that "whatever the end shall be (and of this we can have no idea) justifies whatever we are doing."

The unknown cannot justify anything.

X X I

THE MORE WE assume about the future, the less we understand the present.

Kildare Dobbs, author of *Running to Paradise*, told me the other day, "I've been trying to get rid of my foresight for years!"

X X I I

EXPERTS, LIKE demented old Gypsy women, consult the cards of their computers and tell us that only two percent of mankind will be working in the year 2000.

They pick up another card and shake their heads gravely. Our electric needs must be doubled in every decade (it seems we don't have enough electric eggbeaters, car-plane-bomb-missile factories) and we have no choice but to build nuclear power plants; it's inevitable. We simply must produce enough undisposable radioactive waste to wipe out whole nations through a couple of accidents and, in the meantime, heat up and poison the rivers, our food, the air. It's regrettable, of course—but to satisfy our future needs we must hasten our deaths.

Such men, high on the future-drug, are celebrated as the greatest authorities and sages.

X X I I I

OUR WHOLE civilization is based on a hypothetical future and the idiocy of fortune-telling.

X X I V

WHEN SOMEONE tells you "you must think of the future," he isn't thinking of you.

X X V

WHEN YOU HEAR the word "inevitable," watch out! An enemy of humanity has identified himself.

X X V I

IF PEOPLE assumed the existence of an orderly world and a predictable and controllable future simply because they hadn't given the matter sufficient thought, the philosophy of our age would never have caught on. What is involved here is not so much ideas as our emotional attitudes.

We're mortal, so we conceive immortality; we live in continuous change, so we conceive permanence. The stress of living in chaos is intolerable, so we conceive order. It is reassuring.

The unchangeable laws of nature appeal to us because they have a solidity that our lives lack. There is a story that Galileo stamped the ground and cried *"Eppure si muove!"* after he withdrew his discoveries to appease the Inquisition. If so, there was more to his outburst than mere stubborn pride in his science: he must have found consolation in the knowledge that however cowardly and inconstant he had been, the earth was rotating just the same. Contemplating such changeless truths gives one an uplifting sense of eternity.

We're imprisoned in the human span, and our longing to extend ourselves into the future is irrepressible. Whenever the future is evoked, we can feel the sort of thrill we experience looking at the ocean. The huge expanse of water seems endless and timeless; it expands our souls beyond our limits. I've never watched the sea without being comforted by the thought that the breakers had been surging toward the shore for millions of years and would go on unceasingly forever. At such moments the prospect of dying seems natural and easy to accept.

We need a sense of order, which assures us of continuity, to be able to live with our death.

X X V I I

MOREOVER, we envisage an orderly world to fit our orderly plans. We cannot help feeling that our aims and activities influence events more decisively than random bricks falling from rooftops. But if everything ultimately depends on coincidence (on the convergence of otherwise unrelated events), if each situation is filled with innumerable and therefore unknowable possibilities, then we can neither forecast the future nor manage our lives.

So in all this the big issues of the ego are at stake. The question of how events occur is really the question of our freedom and power.

Napoleon in His Study by David, National Gallery of Art, Washington, D.C. (CULVER PICTURES, INC.)

Rule Number Two

POWER WEAKENS
AS IT GROWS

I USED TO KNOW a young man who had the misfortune to be repulsive. I don't know where he is now or what he is doing; at the time, he was trying to sell vacuum cleaners or encyclopedias in Montreal, though it was difficult to imagine anyone buying anything from a salesman with such a froglike appearance. Short, frail, yet prematurely potbellied, he had a small, bony head, which was always slightly tilted and seemed overpowered by two large, bulging, glaucous eyes. To make matters worse, it was evident that he seldom washed, and he was of course poor.

We used to eat in the same inexpensive café on Stanley Street, and one evening when the place was full he sat at my table. From then on he came over whenever he saw me, to talk about his frustrations and longings, concerning mainly women.

Some time after we met, he decided to covet a pretty "singer" whom I knew slightly—I'll call her Chantal. She was the kind of artistic, sensitive girl who despises the commercial rat race of the modern world but happens to be kept by an unhappy businessman with a lot of money. Not that Chantal was a kept woman in the ordinary sense. To emphasize her independence, she made a point of having brief, passionate affairs, free of charge, with other men, preferably young and handsome executives with Jaguars. Still, by the time her rent and charge accounts were due she always happened to make up with her patron, who was reassured that she preferred him to all other men and gladly paid the bills.

Clearly, my friend had nothing to offer to such a swinging bitch.

"I've fallen in love with that girl," he told me one evening at the café, his bulging eyes protruding even further. "I'm going to screw her."

I tried to dissuade him from his plans, to save him from humiliation. Chantal was good-looking, even perhaps beautiful, and she had known a great many men who had everything she wanted. Her thick, black hair falling loosely to her waist created the impression that she was susceptible to such spontaneous emotions as sympathy and generosity, but the free-floating mane was a cover, not a sign. I have never been more certain of anything about the future than of the self-evident fact that there was not going to be anything between those two.

"Don't worry," he insisted, "I've got it all worked out. I can do anything if I really put my mind to it—I'll make her."

He did. Chantal's comment on this baffling event was widely quoted in the Montreal cafés. "I wanted to know what it was like to make love with an absolute creep," she said. "I've never had sex with nausea before."

The seducer, uninformed, was profoundly pleased with himself. He had accomplished what he set out to do; he was a man who got things done. He thought that he had succeeded because he was so ingenious and persistent, because his passion, his pleadings, his ploys were irresistible.

However, Chantal refused to see him again, let alone go to bed with him, and he was plunged into despairing confusion. He had been so clever at getting her, so conscientious in making sure that she had her orgasm. What could have gone wrong? He was convinced that somewhere, somehow, he had made a fatal mistake. Just as he had taken pride in a freakish chance, so afterward he blamed himself for his bad luck. In addition to all his other miseries, he suffered the torments of guilt.

I I

MAKE A DATE for tonight, for tomorrow, for a week from now, for a year from now. Make a date for ten years from now!

The effectiveness of your will to achieve your aims diminishes with the extension of time. Time works to put you down. If you ask him for a short loan, he is likely to oblige without bothering you too much. But he soon gets impatient, restless, and interfering.

Time is not unlike a child on the beach—you tell him to stay put, drink his Coke, build his sand castle, *eat* his sand castle, but for heaven's sake keep still, don't get into trouble, dad needs a rest. But despite all exhortations he'll grow restless and will keep running away and coming back, bringing down on you an inattentive matron's bikini top, an amateur photographer's Rollei, two rubber crocodiles, an alcoholic's hip flask, a tube of suntan lotion, an outraged young man's Italian sunglasses, three beach balls of different colors and the lifeguard's whistle. What has all this got to do with you? Nothing. Yet a great many angry strangers are going to converge on you, spoiling your chances to acquire a tan in peace.

But things are getting too hectic for childish analogies; let's borrow from physics to understand history.

As THERE IS NO TIME without place and no place without time, the extension of either will extend both, thus increasing the interference of chance in our affairs.

the convergence of
otherwise unrelated $=$ *time + place* $=$ *chance*
events

$$\mathrm{TIME} + \text{place} = \mathrm{TIME} + \mathrm{PLACE} = \mathrm{CHANCE}$$

$$\text{time} + \mathrm{PLACE} = \mathrm{TIME} + \mathrm{PLACE} = \mathrm{CHANCE}$$

$$\mathrm{TIME} + \mathrm{PLACE} = \mathrm{CHANCE}$$

I V

THE NUMBER of possible and actual occurrences increases with time, so that the extension of time alone will involve progressively more people and events over a wider area—in short, will involve also an extension of place.

Now I'm not sure which is more confusing, abstractions or parables, but let me again try an example. A thief comes to your house and points a gun at your nose, ordering you to collect all your loose cash. The space apparently involved is only your house; and if the gunman is fast and clears out in ten minutes, that appearance may hold good. But as you are part of humanity and the world is in continuous motion, other people and thus other places are also involved with you, even while you're alone, and as time passes the relevance of these other people and places will increase. In the first ten minutes, probably no one will phone you or drop by, but as time *spreads* (it spreads rather than flows) a friend may call, the milkman ring with the weekly bill, another member of the family come home and let himself in with his own key, catching the thief off guard. In truth, criminals are good philosophers. No armed burglar intends to stay at your house for twenty-four hours—he knows too well that he cannot "localize the conflict," cannot limit the situation if it is prolonged. He understands that his power to dominate the scene is dissipating, that his weapon is shrinking in size in relation to the spreading situation—so he knows that if he doesn't hurry, he is going to get caught.

The fast thinker who has turned the example around interrupts to point out that time may have shrunk the thief, but it "built up" the innocent householder. Untrue, my friend. At the moment of the gunman's arrival, the intended victim's reaction (his bravery, his agility in grabbing the weapon) was nearly as significant as the gunman's intention to get the money. But as time passes and what happens outside becomes more relevant, it matters less and less how tough is the thief and how brave the victim. What matters is whether his old friend will drop by. It is true, of course, that the weaker party benefits from the stronger party's loss of control—but this isn't the same thing as to say that the weaker party grows stronger.

Time cuts down everybody's power—time is on the side of chance.

V

Go, sir, gallop, and don't forget that the world was made in six days. You can ask me for anything you like, except time.

Napoleon—to an aide (1803)

AN AMERICAN MAGAZINE has arranged for me an interview with the former Emperor, so I may ask him to elaborate on his statement. After a great deal of red tape, it was agreed that I might join him on his walk in the gardens of Fontainebleau, where he periodically reappears, strictly as a visitor, of course. Although officially he is entitled only to his military rank, General Bonaparte is still addressed as *sire* by his aides and admirers and referred to as *l'empereur.* Those who are interested in the habits of the great man may be pleased to learn that he still holds his right arm inside his coat and is fond of the brandy named after him.

The Emperor had to search his memory to recall his remark about the timetable of creation, but once he started talking, his remarks were delivered with brisk impatience.

"The Almighty had no choice," he said. "If He hadn't created the world in six days, He could never have done it. If He had taken but a day longer, something was bound to go wrong."

"Which is why, Sire, you were willing to grant people anything but time?"

He freed his right arm from his coat and made a gesture as if to brush aside any implied compliment. "Since Alexander the Great, every commander has been aware that time deploys more and more forces against him, places more and more obstacles in his way. His troops become less useful to him by the day, even if there are no casualties."

"According to Count Tolstoy, Sire, General Kutuzov was of a different opinion. He thought time was on his side and, as you may remember . . ."

"*Bien sûr*, I was beaten in Russia, in 1812 or 1813, if I recall correctly; it was a long time ago. Of course, Kutuzov had home-time and I had to work on foreign-time—that makes some difference, *monsieur*. Besides, Kutuzov knew that I had troublemakers back home, demagogues kept asking, 'What do we need Russia for?' It wasn't Kutuzov who beat me, but the situation."

"But that's just it, Sire—the developing situation did help General Kutuzov."

"For a while, yes—he could afford to wait around for a few months, even for a year or so. But I am sure if there had been any sign that I could keep my troops there for years, General Kutuzov would have hurried up. A little time could help him—*mais des années—des années!* In a few years his soldiers might have mutinied—there could have been a *révolution*, sweeping away the Czar, Kutuzov, the whole despotic regime. In truth, I did hope for a revolution in Russia, but I had even less time than they did to wait it out."

I explained to the Emperor about the Vietnam War and all the trouble it was creating in the States, and happened to mention that President Nixon, like President Johnson before him, was asking the American public for "more time."

"*Bien entendu, les politiciens sont capables de demander n'importe quoi!*" (But of course—politicians are capable of asking for anything.)

"But it isn't just the politicians, Sire. They are asking for more time because their generals are asking them for it."

"This I refuse to believe," General Bonaparte said flatly.

"*Pas de bêtises!*" (Don't talk nonsense!) "If you ask for more time you're asking for more trouble. Every general knows that."

"Perhaps I'm not making myself clear, Sire. America is a stronger and bigger country than it used to be. And besides, you know, there have been tremendous advances in technology. The Americans have a ten-ton bomb for every tree in the jungle over there."

The Emperor shook his head. "It is never a question of troops and weapons, but of the whole situation and how long it lasts. Your Americans may be stronger than General de Gaulle keeps telling me, but believe me, *monsieur*, even if they were as strong and powerful as the armies of Alexander the Great—there is just no power, no force which can conquer the territory of a decade. *Ça, c'est beaucoup de terrain.*"

(place + T I M E = P L A C E + T I M E)

"I will tell you a Russian proverb that I heard when I was over there and have never forgotten, for reasons you can imagine. The Russians say, 'Time is like the great steppes: if you advance too far into it, you are bound to get lost.'"

It was time to change the subject. "How do you explain, Sire," I asked, "that you were so successful as a commander-in-chief, yet had nothing but . . . I mean, had quite a lot of trouble as an emperor?"

"Battles, *monsieur*," Napoleon said, his face looking suddenly old, "battles do not take long, they are a question of hours or days. But to rule, *hélas!* It takes time to rule." He added with melancholy hindsight: "That is why history has had so many victors and so few rulers."

The Emperor was evidently growing weary of politics and wished to end the interview. We had just come around to one of the most charming gardens at Fontainebleau, the Jardin de Diane. Guarded by four magnificent bronze hounds, the goddess of the hunt strides forward on her round column, reaching over her shoulder with one hand to pluck an arrow from her quiver, while the other caresses the head of a fawn leaping by her side. The Emperor paused for a moment to rest his eyes on the divine huntress. (It was here, in the Jardin de Diane, that he used to walk while recovering from his suicide attempt, in the spring of 1814.)

Before dismissing me, the Emperor favored me with one last remark. "No matter where you fight, *cher monsieur*, even if it is in the Sahara—if the campaign lasts too long, the Russian winter is bound to set in."

V I

IF IT STRUCK YOU that the odds against Napoleon getting Russia were greater than the odds against you getting yourself an apartment with an extra room, then you're ready for the essential truth about human power.

To be sure, the "rulers" of the world have the power to do a great many things you and I are unable to do (they can live rich and can have a lot of people killed), and for this reason we tend to assume that they have a correspondingly greater power over affairs of state than you or I have over our personal affairs. In fact the exact opposite is true.

Let's make the pleasant assumption that you have been promoted. What happens when you rise in power? As a simple member of the planning department, you had to suffer the impertinence of a colleague and could do nothing about it; now that you have become the head, you can fire the guy. You can indulge your vengeance, you're getting better paid, you find you have the talent to make people see your point, you've become funny and penetrating; you believe every word you have ever heard about the glory of power. The only thing is—your job has become more difficult.

Previously you had to worry only about what you were doing yourself: you received a forecast for ten million new babies next year, so you passed on a request for two hundred thousand more law enforcement officers. The whole affair had nothing more to do with you; you took out the secretary and had a good time. But now, while you've acquired the power to fire another man, you also find that you've become dependent on all those who remain. They admire and love you, they're willing to die for you, but they get sick and stay home, or they come in late, they waste time, their work isn't done properly (though you won't even learn about most of the things that go wrong until it is too late). Of course it's also possible that your subordinates will happen to do a good job, and your reorganization of the department may even be helpful to them. However, the fact remains that your control over what is being done with the papers heaped on a hundred desks is going to be considerably less than the control you exercised over the IN and OUT trays on a single desk in your days as a humble employee—when you didn't have to worry about the presence, sanity and performance of a great many other people.

This is not an appeal for sympathy on behalf of men

with annual salaries of 150,000 dollars, but a reminder that what they have got is more money.

Power involves its lucky possessors in ever-expanding situations over which they can exercise ever-decreasing control.

My chances of getting myself a glass of water are greater than my chances of bringing ten thousand people to turn on the tap. The greater the scope of one's activity (that is, the greater one's power) the less is one's ability to influence events.

V I I

A MOST SIGNIFICANT fact to grasp about power (i.e., enforcing your will—to conquer Russia or to get yourself a bigger apartment) is that to succeed you must dominate more than people, you must dominate the situation, the sum total of events.

Whenever we try to overcome an obstacle or an adversary, we tend to assume that we are involved in a direct conflict: it's all between us and the enemy, we'll walk down on Main Street, shoot it out, and that will be the *end of it*. A particularly poignant example of this is "confrontation." I can perceive the Gary Cooper look under both the Che Guevara beret and the riot-squad helmet. The participants may have read their Marx or their Barry Goldwater, but before all else they were brainwashed by a thousand Westerns—Hollywood turned out to be a most poisonous influence, not so much by its obvious absurdities or even its violence, but by mass-communicating misconceptions about how life works. One of the worst misconceptions (we're in the business of detecting murderous notions) which is shared by many millions is the notion of direct conflict—the notion that it's all a question of your power and their power, and may the better power win.

Sharing this insane presumption with most of their contemporaries, President Kennedy got the United States into Vietnam, President Johnson escalated the war, and President Nixon has kept it going—the illusion of direct conflict makes it impossible to perceive that one can be defeated even if one is stronger than the "enemy." And meanwhile, back in the cities, militant protesters and police are marching to confront each other. That is what chaos is all about, you see, the convergence of otherwise unrelated events— who could have foreseen that Gary Cooper, walking so straight and tall, would lead America into an ambush?

In real life there is never such a thing as a "direct conflict" on an empty Main Street, between opposing armies, between you and the boss, or even between you and a girl; it isn't a question of one's ingenuity, charm, or gun against another's, so it isn't a question of who is better and stronger—or rather, this is an issue which rapidly loses its relevance as time goes on.

V I I I

WEAPONS ARE MEANS of destruction, not means of control. The real enemy is the situation, and it cannot be gunned down or arrested, it can only be trailed.

Here again we can take our clue from the successful criminal, who could teach presidents a thing or two, for he cannot go by Hollywood, he must know how things work in life as otherwise he will go to jail. I hate to remind you of the gunman who dropped by to pick up your valuables, but "it looks as if we overlooked an important clue," says private-eye-extraordinary Philip Marlowe. The clever criminal doesn't see the robbery as a direct conflict between you and himself, he doesn't think that his being armed has much to do with his chances of success. He doesn't worry about dominating you: he is stronger than you, he has the gun; if you obey him, fine; if you don't, he'll shoot you, that's not his problem. His problem is *what happens next*. While you're still holding up your hands nicely, he is checking the silencer on his gun, he is busy cutting the telephone cord, drawing the curtains: he is trying to dominate the *situation*, because he knows that his enemy is the situation, not you. And as we have already noted, he is also clever enough to know that, regardless of his weapons, no man can dominate the situation of rapidly multiplying occurrences for long, so he will clear out as fast as possible.

Political leaders can be likened to the stupid criminal who doesn't understand that getting away with the loot won't depend on how successfully he intimidates his victim, but on what will happen next, on the totality of occurrences—and who believes that the decisive thing is his firepower.

And isn't this the way we all tend to think about the powerful, their armies, their police, their secret police? Or the rebels' guns?

I X

As IN HUMAN affairs many of the events arise from deliberate actions (albeit from their haphazard convergence), it is worthwhile to differentiate between people and their actions if we are to see the hole in the mighty's armor, the leak in the Molotov cocktail.

Let's say that martial law is established and you, as the head of the planning department, have acquired absolute power and can not only fire your subordinates, but can also have them shot if they disobey your orders. Will this increase your actual control over the department? It will increase your control over your subordinates' intentions—they will be scared and they will do their utmost to perform to your satisfaction. They won't come in late, they won't spend time chatting and drinking coffee, they will raise their fists in unison and cry, "Long Live Kosygin!" or "Long Live Spiro Agnew!"—and if you instituted terror just to see people suffer, you can indeed be satisfied that extra power gives you an extra chance to indulge your peculiar kinks. But if we're talking about *purposeful terror*, employed not to make people suffer but to achieve specific aims, like a better planning department according to your directions, you'll find that your introduction of terror has in fact decreased your effective control. People may wish to please you more, but the very fact that they're scared and nervous is likely to impair their performance. For one thing, many of them will start drinking and come in every morning with hangovers. They will be so keen to obey your orders, not to be at fault, that they will blunder out of overeagerness. Moreover, they'll multiply their blunders by trying to cover them up for dear life, to put the blame on someone else—often successfully. And you'll never even know that the man you shot as a bungling idiot or saboteur was in fact your most competent and faithful clerk.

These hypothetical suggestions (and the whole genesis of my argument about power) originated in my instructive experience of growing up in a police state, the chaotic world of a most tightly oppressed small country, communist Hungary, ruled until 1956 by the dictator Rákosi—a multilingual and well-educated Batista. He had enormous power—including the power (which he exercised) to murder most of the leading figures of his own party, his ministers, the president of the republic and anyone else he happened to think of. But apart from the killing, he had less to do with what went on in the country than the most ineffectual democratic leader. He prevented people from electing the government they wanted, but this did not allow *him* to govern them.

For instance, stealing became a matter of honor. In 1951 Rákosi went to open a big factory in the new town of Stalinváros, only to find on arrival that there was nothing in the place, only empty walls—every machine, every screw, even the doorknobs and windowpanes were missing. As the progress reports went on multiplying while the new factory was in fact diminishing, no one in the chain of command dared to pass a true word upward (a lot of people on the site managed to get themselves transferred the previous year), and so Rákosi did not learn what had happened until he actually went inside the building. You couldn't have less control than that. In this instance the dictator himself must have recognized that terror served him ill, and there were no arrests or executions reported on account of the missing factory. Nonetheless, the whole appalling administrative record of his dictatorship, or of any other you care to take a look at, shows that police states are in fact the worst—or rather the *least*—managed societies.

But at least, you may think wistfully if you're in a foul mood, the dictator had the power to kill anyone he disliked. Yes, but at what a price! By having a great many people killed whom he desperately needed and wanted to stay alive. During the few victorious days of the 1956 revolution, the most shocking discoveries in the files were not the straightforward political murders of communist officials or grumblers, but the private, personal scores which had been settled under the aegis of the fight for socialism. I remember the file on the chief engineer of a big industrial plant—it consisted of a *postcard* from some obscure relative in New York. The man (a highly trained specialist whose skills and experience were of great value to the economy) was executed, which was certainly not in the dictator's interest. Unfortunately, the engineer happened to take away the provincial police chief's girl friend, and the postcard served as a pretext for rubbing out a rival. A dictator cannot even control the direction of violence: through the unavoidable sharing of dictatorial power with its executors he unleashes anarchy in which the local police chiefs roam about freely as armed and capricious bandits in every town.

Far from securing order, terror intensifies disorder and social disintegration. Terror, the most extreme form of power, is the least effective, and rulers employ it to the detriment of their own authority.

As to the most impressive and least real aspect of terror —forcing people to do as they're told—what do *you* do when you want others to perform a task and perform it well? Do you try to scare them? Of course not. "For God's sake," you beg them, "relax, relax!"

Well, then, you've always understood perfectly the weakness of force as a means to rule or control.

X

THIS IS TO STATE the observation that there is a similarity between the dynamics of atoms and the dynamics of human affairs. To perceive this similarity we had best conceive of human power simply as energy and of a situation as a conglomeration of events which are in continuous motion but have a discernible structure and behavior in respect to their mass.

If we could put a situation under a time-space microscope, we could see that its structure (the pattern of the interrelationship of events) is continually changing as the situation expands with the recurrence and recombination of events. This haphazard interrelating is what we call chance.

The term *recurs* is crucial. Events, like atoms, never end—what happens is indestructible. There is no way to undo the slave trade or the French Revolution: if we looked at human affairs under a time-space microscope, we would find these events present here and now, just as we could see the recurring particles of the atom with a miraculous microscope. These particular events (particles) may float freely within the situation and have no significance, but as the pattern of the situation is constantly changing, what was a free-floating event may become the central one in a new configuration. Thus while the enslavement of blacks in America may not have had any visible significance fifteen years ago, it may be in a new structure (a revolution in the United States, let us say) of extreme relevance.

So if we're to understand the behavior of the mass of events, we must not let our watches confuse us—time never passes, it thickens and spreads, for time-space is really a synonym for the mass of events, and this mass of events (just like matter, the mass of atoms) never disappears. Just as whatever was contained in the Earth when it was a gas cloud is still here, so whatever happened since the beginning of human life is still here, interacting with new events as they occur.

Thus a situation always grows in density and also expands; these are the behavioral characteristics of the mass of events.

Now if we could film what we see under our time-space microscope, we could draw a diagram of the chance of that moment. Freezing a split second of time and space, we would find that events interrelated according to their development in the split second before; but we still must call this "structure" the structure of chance, as chance could at any moment rearrange the interrelationship of events in a most drastic manner. We may liken chance to structural energy which (not unlike atomic energy) is at once insignificant and also capable of tearing the world apart.

But while chance itself is subject to chance, it also has the characteristic of increased frequency as the mass of events grows in density and expands. Or to put it in another way, it is the behavioral characteristic of the situation, the mass of events, that it contains an increasingly larger energy of chance, that the haphazardness of the structure is going to become ever more chaotic.

The structural image of a moment of history observed

through a time-space microscope would be the same as what we could observe of a moment of atomic life under a miraculous microscope—something resembling order, something in line with the path of the particles in the previous second. Similarly, as we would adjust our time-space microscope to show us larger and lengthier situations of history, we would get the same structural image as of a larger situation of atomic life—an increasingly chaotic pattern of interrelationships.

Now what remains to be observed is what happens when we apply the energy of human will to the situation, the mass of events. Taking this human energy as the focal point of our observation, we would find that it behaves very much like chance, except in reverse. Chance at the split second of time-place is practically imperceptible—then it continues growing until it presents a picture of chaos. Human power, however, looms large at the beginning, tending to be able to dominate the immediate situation. However! The charge of human energy not only rearranges the structure of the situation (the mass of events), but an effect of this rearrangement is an additional expansion of the situation. So while human power achieves control over certain vital elements within the structure (i.e., achieves its immediate aim), it also expands the situation beyond its control. At the beginning, this tends to have no practical significance. But as more and more human power is applied to the mass of events, we can observe that the situation grows in density and expands at an ever-increasing rate. Moreover, the energy of human power appears to be able to develop only in arithmetical progression, as it were, while the mass of events develops in geometric progression. For example, if human energy increases from one to five, the situation expands from one to twenty-five: the greater the energy applied, the greater the situation, so that maximum power produces maximum situation. Human power which we could measure as fifteen in a situation that could be measured as three hundred is in fact greater than human power which is one hundred in a situation that is ten thousand.

But while the situation, the mass of events, expands at an ever-faster rate under the pressure of human energy to control its structure, it also expands by itself in time-and-space—so that even if we do nothing new, and even if there is no diminution of our strength, at a certain point we inescapably begin to lose control—a process which goes to the point of zero.

X I

To UNDERSTAND the exact relationship between our activities and the results, we ought to recall again the devious behavior of chance: it seldom asserts itself in a drastic manner within a brief space of time.

Though you cannot predict with absolute assurance what will happen in the next second, it is likely that you will be able to accomplish most of the reasonably modest tasks you set yourself.

Barring great accidents in his personal life, it is possible for an unobservant person to live through every day of his life in the belief that he is actually in control of his small personal world. But if he were to look back over a long period—say twenty-five years—he would have to realize that the unexpected turns that chance brought into the course of his life, which were too small for him even to notice at the time, did make a great deal of difference and that he isn't at all where he intended to be (whether he's better off or worse). He may have felt every day of his life that he was in control, but it is impossible for him to see himself as having controlled twenty-five years of his life—the discrepancy between his intentions and the results is just too glaring, the unrelated events which altered his twenty-five-year situation are too apparent to ignore.

Another way of putting this is to say that it is possible for us to dominate a small and brief situation, but impossible to dominate a "large" situation.

Thus your success in any endeavor depends mainly on how large the situation is, rather than on your own power—or to be more exact, it depends on the relative balance between the weight you can pull and the weight of the situation which you are trying to dominate. Your chances of pushing through a program of university reform are fairly high. Your chances of starting a revolution are nil—or rather, it won't depend on anything you can do. Chance can always reverse this relationship between a man's efforts and the size of the situation, but the kind of combination of events that could allow for it recurs less often than an all-night win at a roulette table.

But to take a more familiar example of how chance tends to manifest itself: though you needed your cleverness and the power of your irresistible charm to succeed with a girl, all your qualities will count for progressively less in having a successful relationship with her—and this on account of events which, strictly speaking, have nothing to do with either of you (she has to go to work, her boss is mean to her and puts her in a bad mood, or he suddenly becomes all too nice to her, the building next door to you is being demolished and your bedroom shakes most unnervingly, an old girl friend calls, and so on). It is the constant reduction of the relevance of our intentions and actions as the situation grows which accounts for the fact that practically everybody succeeds in getting married but few succeed in marriage. I can give you in a sentence the combined wisdom of all the how-to-succeed books: aim at something which will take the least possible time and will involve the smallest number of people.

X I I

VIOLENCE IS the most extreme manifestation of human will, and it writes large a self-defeating tendency inherent in all our attempts to impose our will on events—which is that our action expands the situation and intensifies it.

Here comes our old friend the gunman, holding you up on a dark, deserted street, just for a change. On this occasion he is already fleeing from the police, and so his situation is already expanding by itself through time and his movements. But by exerting violence against you, he puts himself in additional danger by involving you, the neighborhood and possibly a cruising police car. In this more dangerous situation the relevance of his past record acquires new significance, and so does the relevance of your past—whether, for instance, you have taken judo lessons. By interfering with you, by placing himself in your path, he is also placing himself in the path of your judo lessons. A lot of things about you and the environs, which otherwise would have nothing whatever to do with him, become most relevant to his future. And yet any ruler could envy the criminal for the odds in his favor.

Napoleon himself demonstrated most strikingly the

power of both revolutionary and state violence. As a general of the Revolution, he could seize power in France with incredible ease, and at first the expansion of the situation only increased the effectiveness of his troops. The French supported him for restoring public order and for defending their liberties against the rapacious monarchies of the rest of Europe. His violence against Austrian armies gained him not only military victories, but also the enthusiastic support of the Habsburgs' oppressed subjects—he was the hero of not only France, but Austria and Italy as well. All this soon made him so powerful that he involved with himself the whole of Europe, multiplying the odds against him to the point where the strength and enthusiasm of his troops, his royal relatives, even his own magic no longer counted and he was defeated.

The above pattern can be observed in any human situation, small or great. Yet historians, politicians, and individuals keep saying, "If only this or that hadn't happened." With the whole of human history behind them, they are unable to perceive that it is the nature of our world that things keep happening.

To say "I'm getting involved" is to tell the happy part of the story. When you get involved, a great many things are getting involved with *you*.

The more people you kill, the less good it does you.

X I I I

By ALL MEANS, let's despise the powerful, but let's not imitate their madness. Let's learn the nature of our strength from the undignified and contemptible spectacle of men trying to play gods.

As time expands with space just as much as space expands with time, an authoritarian ruler has as much control over one day in the lives of two thousand of his subjects as a humble citizen has over twenty-five years of his life.

Power weakens as it grows, because the level of chaos rises as a situation expands.

X I V

"But what about the power of great nations—isn't there strength in numbers?"

"Forget it. Let's take a sex-break."

X V

The sad glamor of masturbation is that it is simpler than making love. The complexities of one person's relationship to himself don't begin to compare with the complexities of a couple's romance. Similarly, a triangle is more than three times as complicated as a twosome—there are many more misunderstandings, mix-ups, conflicts. As for a wife-swapping relationship of twenty people, it's bound to be a most chaotic affair.

The historical significance of all this is not sufficiently appreciated.

X V I

When interviewed by Edgar Snow in 1961, Chairman Mao Tse-tung was irritated by Snow's reminder that

China's population was getting close to a thousand million people. One would have thought that the number of his subjects would have pleased Mao as much as it frightens many Western observers, who talk about the "Chinese giant" as a great threat to Asia and the rest of the world by the sheer size of its population. Yet this indication of enormous power didn't seem to impress Mao, it wasn't one of the things he wanted to threaten paper tigers with—on the contrary, he insisted that the estimates were exaggerated, that the census didn't take into account all those who must have died. Evidently he was unnerved by the possibility that he would have to rule nearly a thousand million people—or (never mind ruling) would have the task of simply holding together an ocean of human beings. I'm certain it was this terrifying prospect that inspired the idea of the little red book: let them recite it day and night, let at least a few dozen million of them march up and down the avenues, shaking paper. At least while they were marching and shouting they wouldn't be getting up to any mischief—although things didn't work out quite that way either.

One of Mao's thoughts missing from the printed text must be that after all the fighting, all the talk of organization, all the trouble of setting up a dictatorial regime, there is still no way of governing with any certainty or in any effective manner nearly one billion people. Despite the decrees, the party apparatus (but what is the party apparatus up to, itself bigger than many fair-sized nations!), the army (!), the police, there is nothing strong enough to hold the Chinese together—unless it is the Word.

A professor who had spent some time in the Kennedy

administration and never recovered from reviewing military parades as if he were a general, lectured me once about the threat of China swallowing the rest of Asia. I'll never understand how a man can become a Harvard professor without even knowing that Chinese emperors have been trying for the last three thousand years to swallow *China*—an occupation which no doubt will keep them busy for the next three thousand years, if nothing untoward happens in the meantime.

I'm sure a few hundred officials within the smallest inner circle of the Heavenly Palaces have toyed with the notion of killing the old chairman by convincing him that the government of India had quit, inviting China to take over, and that he had just no way of refusing the gift of 450 million additional subjects.

X V I I

To SOME DEGREE tensions, conflicts, sheer confusion tend to make human relationships livelier, challenging people to fuller and more active self-realization. A lover is obviously a more fully realized person than an onanist, a family with only one child is likely to be weaker than a family with several children, and Andorra is evidently too small to be a dynamic nation.

Yet whatever kind of human group we look at, we'll see that beyond a certain point the law of diminishing returns begins to operate. As communities continue to grow past their optimum size, they become less coherent, looser, more discordant. It appears, in fact, that the biggest nations constitute the sickest, and thus the weakest, societies in the world, resembling nothing so much as listless or hate-filled orgies with a lot of alcohol being consumed.

It is true that no one could ever really conquer and occupy China or the Soviet Union or (whatever the Minutemen may fear) the United States, so in this sense they are "strong." However, a huge country seems unconquerable for the very reason why her own citizens can never quite manage to conquer her.

X V I I I

THE HISTORICAL evidence for the strength of the biggest countries is not very impressive.

Despite the fact that China had a long head start on European civilization, it has forever remained a weak and divided country with frequent relapses into anarchy. Moreover, China, like other big nations, has the weakness of being insulated from the rest of the world: people who live in such a huge community that they cannot possibly relate to it don't seem to be able to relate to the whole of mankind either. There is such a thing as imperial provincialism, and it is the thickest, isn't it, my poor friends in New York and Moscow!

The most dynamic continent in the world has been Europe—a continent which, but for the periodic plagues of empires, consisted of many small countries.

The city-states of Florence, Venice and papal Rome were stronger on their own than united Italy has ever managed to be—and I mean stronger in terms of their culture, their community life, the freedom and happiness of their citizens. The German principalities were among the most prosperous, liberal and civilized communities in Europe—light-years ahead of gigantic Russia. And they knew it. Prussia's Bismarck didn't get very far with his idea of unification until Ludwig II of Bavaria went mad and signed away his kingdom. The Germans have had nothing but trouble ever since. Their tragedy isn't the fact that there are two Germanies, but that there are only two.

X I X

NATIONS, like young girls, are unhappy if they get too big.

Large countries contain large passions—of fear, jealousy and hate. There are no big countries without ineradicable grievances. To be better understood, I should be saying this in the language of the Tartars or the Ibos.

In the past two and a half years, over two million Biafrans were starved or killed for the sake of a united Nigeria, and the madmen who try to rule the world rejoice in the restoration of still another miserable and chaotic superstate.

Yet who knows what the future may hold? Is it too much to hope for tribalization?

Peoples of the world!

d i s p e r s e !

X X

THERE ARE UNIONS which only divide. A world government, far from bringing about universal order and stability, would mean total anarchy.

X X I

Bigness is weakness.

X X I I

THE PIOUS GRUNT that "it's all in God's hands" expressed a far more pragmatic notion of how events occur than the modern presumption that man can calculate and control his destiny. The abolition of the Deity turned out to be only a palace revolution after all. We haven't abandoned the idea of an omnipotent and omniscient being, we are just trying to fill this nonexistent role ourselves—both in our personal lives and in history.

We pay a high price for this folly. Our attempts to wield decisive (godlike) control over events are the source of private neurosis and public horror.

If Throughout His Reign Napoleon . . .

IT WOULD be difficult to find anyone obsessed by the fact that the sun sets in the evening. Obsessions grow from uncertainties. To believe in something which one suspects may not be true is to begin to disregard the evidence of one's senses, to grow stubborn against the facts.

We've been conditioned by the economic religions of the industrial age, capitalist progressivism and Marxism, to believe in history as a machine, a cause-and-effect mechanism that any expert can fix. We plan our lives by this myth, we're governed in its name—yet we're not altogether ignorant of its absurdity. We cannot be quite unaware of the accidental nature of events, we both know and don't know the odds against imposing our will on life; and it is in such twilight regions of the mind that everything becomes twisted.

The fanatic isn't the man of absolute faith but the believer who has tasted doubt: the early Christians were tolerant even toward their enemies, but as Christianity began to lose its unquestioning innocence, heretics were put to the stake. The learned inquisitors argued that they were obliged to burn people alive to save them from burning in hell. Which didn't make much sense, nor did it need to. The fanatic reasons only to suppress his doubts, to create tangible evidence for the truths of his beliefs, and the stakes were such evidence: real flames could reflect the imaginary flames, the howling and writhing gave substance to the fantasy of torments beyond the grave. Thus otherwise peaceful men set people on fire to affirm their faith in fire everlasting. But if doubt, a speck of common sense, was needed to turn their folly into madness, this was an ironic twist that offers some hope; at any rate, scepticism about hell grew strong enough to restore the mental balance in favor of a symbolic interpretation of the Bible.

Man's faith in a controllable future, however, is still in its medieval stage. The flames of burning flesh leap to high heaven, and doubts inspire only firmer resolve to daydream and to kill.

Who doesn't remember President Lyndon B. Johnson's dreams about Vietnam? his projects for building up the country even while he was issuing orders for its destruction? his conviction that he would make Vietnam a warning example to all foes of freedom and the American empire, even after it was apparent that the example would not impress even the Vietnamese?

In fact all of Johnson's aims turned into fantasies, with only a dreamlike connection to reality, once it became manifest that none of his objectives could be realized and the war held no victories, only losses. Yet throughout his reign he persisted with the unprofitable carnage, which was wrecking his own country as well as his personal career. The puzzle of Johnson's presidency will outlive its horror.

Yet if we are puzzled, it is because of the way we have been taught history, the way the papers serve us our daily news of suffering and death, as if history were a common-sense enterprise in which leaders, vile or noble, clever or not so clever, create hell on earth for sound reasons.

It was a telling point of the war that whatever vituperation and explosives the adversaries were exchanging, they repeatedly gave each other a clean bill of mental health. Despite the fact that the North Vietnamese and Vietcong leaders showed just as much fortitude about the suffering of the Vietnamese people as President Johnson himself, he often assured us that they were "bound to come to their senses." They inexplicably returned the compliment by claiming that they were forcing Johnson and his fellow imperialists to "face up to the facts." Neither Marxism nor Western libertarianism had prepared them (or us, the spectators) to recognize that men may be—and usually are—influenced more by their passionate illusions than by rational self-interest.

Indeed, the supposition that people are bound to respond rationally to our actions accounts for more suffering than even wars could contain. It accounts for the silent rage that burns longer than napalm and hurts almost as badly, the rage of bitter disappointment that turns lovers into miserable couples and ruins our talent for happiness, even in quiet corners of the world.

But then, the reader can say, wishing to get back to the point, we're told that men are aggressive animals and senseless wars are caused by our cruel instincts. Yet it is difficult to see how even a sadist could enjoy high-altitude bombing, let alone issuing orders for such bombing at a great distance, far from the scene of blood and screams. The currently fashionable notion of man's extreme cruelty tells us little about history, apart from our preference to see ourselves as excitingly bestial rather than just plain unbalanced—and unbalanced for the less than fascinating reason that we harbor false notions about ourselves.

Men kill like sleepwalkers: their daydreams protect them from realizing what they're doing. So even when the absurdity of his enterprise began to dawn on the President, he could convince himself that he had no choice but to carry on the senseless war until the North Vietnamese decided to let him off the hook by being sensible themselves. ("Why should *I* be the one to stop screaming?" a couple kept shouting at each other in the block where I used to live, waking the neighborhood in the middle of the night.) Johnson's warning pleas to his adversaries followed the classic pattern of obsession: he insisted on give-and-take, on reciprocity, as if he were saying, "You'll have to come to your senses, because I won't unless you do, and if you won't, we're both in trouble."

The notion that the President of the United States needed Hanoi's agreement—Hanoi's permission, as it were —to end a disastrous war infuriated many of his native critics, who accused him and his aides of cynically misleading the public. Yet no one who observed them on television could doubt their sincerity. The rationalizations which protect a dream are part of the dream: not being able to tear themselves away from the enemy, they saw themselves standing up to him—and did so with genuine grief for all those who would never stand up again on account of the quiet determination of their leaders. No P.R. stance was involved here. The protestations of powerlessness to step outside the power struggle over Vietnam, uttered in tones of dignified detachment by men who were so passionately involved that their conscience no longer reacted to the horrors they were inflicting, and the looks of sorrowful innocence and regret were just as compulsive as the burning of Vietnam.

Every obsession carries its tail end of reverse feeling—didn't Eichmann think highly of Jewish culture? Whether he is obsessed with exterminating a race or pursuing a woman beyond reach or beating the little brown Reds, when the victim is no longer able to control his involvement, then he needs at least the illusion that he is still in charge of himself; and the greater the obsession, the more compelling is the need for unrelated or opposite feelings to allow him a sense of freedom despite his enslavement. The alcoholic on all fours insists that though he drinks he is sober all the time—he drinks, in fact, only to be able to think straight—he wouldn't touch the stuff if it made him drunk. The American language has the apt phrase: *genuine phony*.

I personally became convinced that President Johnson and his advisers were running amok when they began to manifest a deep-seated desire to see themselves standing still, which was about the only thing they were evidently *not* doing.

How could otherwise sane men come to such a pass? How could millions mistake such irrational behavior for statesmanship? The latter question implicates the basic assumptions of our age. It is more convenient, of course, just to forget about the whole thing, but while the characters disappear with the day, the nightmare remains with us, as long as we believe in absolute human power. The truth is that power (in the sense individuals long for it and "the powerful" are assumed to have it) is a mirage; and it is in the pursuit of mirages that people lose their minds.

"Power is a word the meaning of which we do not understand," wrote Tolstoy in *War and Peace:*

> If throughout his reign Napoleon continues to issue commands concerning an invasion of England and expends on no other undertaking so much time and effort, and yet during his whole reign never once attempts to execute his design but undertakes an expedition to Russia, with which country, according to his repeatedly expressed conviction, he considers it to his advantage to be in alliance—then this results from the fact that his commands did not correspond to the course of events in the first case but did so in the latter.
>
> For a command to be carried out to the letter it must be a command actually capable of fulfillment. But to know what can and what cannot be carried out is impossible, not only in the case of Napoleon's invasion of Russia, in which millions participated, but even in the case of the simplest event, seeing that both the one and the other are liable at any moment to find themselves confronted by millions of obstacles. Every command executed is always one of an immense number unexecuted. All commands inconsistent with the course of events are impossible and do not get carried out. Only the possible ones link up into a consecutive series of commands corresponding to a series of events, and are carried out.

No wonder presidents and prime ministers can speak with some feeling about the limitations of power. But speaking of the "limits" of power is still twisting a painful truth to fit a delusion. The fact is that even the most powerful men, far from being in the enviable position of lacking the means to do everything they want in the world, cannot be *certain* of their ability to achieve *any* of their aims. Politics is indeed the art of the possible, except that one can only guess what is possible. If throughout his reign Napoleon issued commands which were to lead to the invasion of England, yet invaded Russia instead—if the Soviet and American leaders acted in 1956 to pacify the Middle East and increase their own influence with the Arab States—if Nasser closed the Gulf of Aqaba to weaken Israel—if successive American presidents issued orders to bring peace, prosperity, and security to South Vietnam—then it must be concluded that when a man wields power he has little notion of what he is actually doing. Not because he is necessarily stupid, but because his authority relates him to such an immense number of possibilities: events that may or may not occur will cancel out his commands or thwart their execution or alter their effect or sometimes (and this is the tantalizing part of it) crown them with success. To have power is to experience chaos, the core of human existence—which creates such a deep sense of uncertainty, such an abiding conviction that *anything* is possible, that the men around President Kennedy, some of the best-informed officials in the country, could believe that the assassination was part of a communist conspiracy to take over the United States. The "limitation" of power is that it is a nightmare.

While the traditional Eastern response to the chaos of life has been inertia, the traditional Western reaction has been to ignore the nature of life (the flux of billions of laws and occurrences) and to behave as if we could impose our will upon events, as if we could command the future.

Taking chances, we were bound to be lucky now and then, if in limited ways; and indeed it is worthwhile to challenge the multitude of contingencies so that the right one *may* occur. But to keep one's sanity one must never lose sight of the fact that one can only try. We must, in Camus's phrase, "act without faith." If events do not echo to our cry of command, we must give up, for *no power on earth can create a single occurrence that is not already a potent possibility.*

The inability of men of power not only to create new realities but even to impose the image of something that does not exist (as opposed to mirages like American or Arab invincibility, which are generated by social and psychological needs) has been analyzed by Hannah Arendt in her essay "Truth and Politics." Despite the all-pervasive mass media at their command, she observes, the news managers achieve the opposite of their intention: the result of all their efforts is that people won't believe even the time of day. "The consistent lying, metaphorically speaking, pulls the ground from under their feet and provides no other ground on which to stand." The powerful can destroy the truth, but they cannot replace it.

Though it was impossible to maintain the image of a Vietnamese society that did not exist, much less bring forth an actual country that wasn't there, Johnson and his colleagues were bent on producing a democratic, friendly, reliable South Vietnam. As they pursued policies based on the decisive and independent efficacy of power—a force in history which is wholly imaginary—they increasingly lost touch with reality and suffered the intellectual and emotional consequences. And this is the process Lord Acton defined as "absolute power corrupts absolutely"—an observation which made Stalin laugh bitterly in one of his sane moments. Camus was nearer the truth in *Caligula:* it was because the emperor could not have the moon that he took leave of his senses. (What horrors are yet to come, now that the moon is within reach while the emperors still cannot grasp the earth!)

Hubris is evidently the mental epidemic of our age, and its germ is the universal daydream that whatever we really, intensely believe to be right and wish and work for must and will happen. In fact most people would shake their heads over an individual who behaved as if he expected his life to take this happy course, but the same people somehow assume that the rules of life change for the benefit of a class or a nation, whose collective destiny unfurls as a huge color-TV spectacular with the right flags filling the screen at the end.

Americans, in particular, still seem to be paying the price for the glory of World War II. They willed to win, they had right and might on their side, they killed and died for victory; how then could they have seen that all this had but a very tenuous connection with the outcome? The whole show seemed so easy to repeat. The British were brought down (or at least closer) to earth by the immediate dissolution of their empire, but the Americans acquired one with less time and effort than they were to expend on the Vietcong. In history nothing fails like success, because it tempts nations to take their good luck for the measure of their strength.

And then there is the notion that, with everything else, power has "progressed"—that the bureaucratic organization of society, industrial wealth, superior weapons have made power *grow*, that it has become more effective than it used to be. But improvements in armaments, communications, technology, science do not change the nature of power, which is potent only when it corresponds to the course of events. Having more of the same unreal thing doesn't make it any more real. Power is still a stick and then the mirage of a stick—now you have it, now you don't—when you have it, it may be a bigger stick, but when you don't, it's just a bigger mirage.

To understand this would be to realize that we can trust God to help those who help themselves only because he likes to play mean practical jokes. To withdraw from Vietnam, Johnson would have had to lose faith in, and then be willing to explode, the myth of power and thus the myth of the United States as "the most powerful nation the world has ever seen." To quit Saigon and acknowledge that the United States could not impose its will on even a small part of a tiny and primitive country would have been to demonstrate the Absurdity of Existence—the problem his experts were trying to solve with computers.

Besides, how could Johnson have shed the delusion of his nation, when most of his critics shared it? They told him that he should use the *immense power* of his office for better purposes! So this great might that everybody was talking about had to exist somewhere, it had to *materialize* with a few more marines, social workers, ambassadors, bombs. But while none of these could turn a single Vietnamese into a Johnson Democrat, the bombs did go off and thereby strengthened his illusion that if he could destroy the world, he must also be able to control it. So he couldn't let go. This was the psychology of escalation, the dynamic of the obsession.

Yet it is difficult to accept, even in retrospect, that a

President of the United States, cheered on by supporters all over the world, was acting out an inner compulsion with half a million soldiers in the field, with thousands dying every week, year after year. If this was possible, we are in deeper trouble than Johnson was in Vietnam. The implications were too much even for the President's bitterest critics; so they argued that Johnson had after all a sane reason to carry on: he was playing the war for personal politics, to win the next election. Little they knew about the integrity of the obsessed! When Senator Eugene McCarthy, running against the President in the New Hampshire primary, demonstrated that Johnson would have to give up either the war or the presidency, Johnson chose the war. He let go of power altogether rather than face up to the fact that he had never had it. This is how men hang on to their obsessions: they would sooner give up a pound of flesh than an ounce of illusion. Moreover, renouncing the highest office, didn't he give the supreme proof of his detachment? Thus reassured, thus freed from the distractions of public protest, indomitably hopeful that his successor would carry on the noble task, he could pursue the mirage to the last day of his reign.

As he often said, he had no choice. The only alternative was a rational one—to stop trying to create events that were not possibilities, realities that did not exist, and dare his people to face the facts of life.

"My fellow Americans," he could have inconceivably said, "I may be the most powerful man in history, but in fact I don't have the power to carry through all the social and economic changes necessary to transform the slums within a five-mile radius of the White House. I could try harder, and I might or might not succeed—there are too

(72)

many imponderables. Remember Prohibition? I couldn't be absolutely certain of success even if I abolished Congress and you accepted me as your dictator with the combined prerogatives of Alexander the Great, Napoleon, Stalin, and Hitler, with a thousand big computers and all the intellectuals working out the details. The only thing certain is that I couldn't make our black citizens more free and equal than the rest of you want them to be.

"Now, as to our efforts to build a new society in the southern part of Vietnam . . .

"As you know, we were fighting there not just on account of that piece of jungle but because we didn't want to hand over control of Southeast Asia to the communists. However, I made a shocking discovery. *There is no such thing as control over Southeast Asia!* Mao nearly started another revolution just to get hold of the control over China, which gave him the slip the first time around, but it seems this dragon doesn't exist either. So I'm giving him one more mirage to pursue: let him and his successors go stark raving mad over it."

But there was, of course, the gun. The only thing real and solid among the floating clouds of unrealities. The guns, the ships, the planes, the bombs, the missiles, the Bomb.

The cruelties of power are the rage of impotence.

David by Bernini, Villa Borghese, Rome (BETTMANN ARCHIVE)

Rule Number Three
IF NOTHING IS CERTAIN, NOTHING IS IMPOSSIBLE

THE PUBLIC forum these arguments are submitted to is my family: Gloria, my wife, and my stepdaughters Martha and Mary, who are the representatives of student power in the house. Both girls agree that Napoleon's power was his luck, while it lasted, and they have no doubt that President Johnson was crazy to think that he could get what he wanted in Vietnam. However, they resent my conclusion that they themselves don't have the power to determine the results of their actions.

"You're advocating passive resistance to life," Martha says, "you do realize that, don't you?" She has long brown hair, wide brown eyes, a firmly passionate character and, at seventeen, is taller than both her mother and myself; she treats us with restrained impatience.

Mary, a slender blonde of fifteen, refuses to fake tolerance: she delivers her opinion with the finality of dismissal. "You say events just happen and we can't be sure of accomplishing anything. So why bother lifting a finger? You're like all the others—you just want to make sure people won't give you any trouble."

There is a note of condescension in her voice which is all too familiar—I had it in my own voice for years. I had such a sharp awareness of everything, such keen senses of touch and sight and smell, I was so filled with life, I had so much more of it than anyone around me: I always found something pathetic in people trying to teach me anything; they were like poor philosophers lecturing a millionaire about money. Why, only a couple of years ago I could still

(77)

imagine myself a wild adolescent! There is no more heavenly sensation over thirty. Men who have their own children have, I suppose, a chance to get used to growing up, but suddenly acquiring grown stepdaughters is a shock —it's like being a boy and aging overnight into an old man. Christ, am I writing this book to convince them that I'm not stupid, even though I'm thirty-five?

But now I'm caught, my age comes up against me: I'm advocating inaction, the virtue of senility.

I fight back. "You're too young and healthy to be so timid about truth. You talk like two old bankers—you want a return even on the facts of life! The proposition that life is chaos and we have no control over the effects of our actions is either true or false, regardless of how we react to it."

"Just the same," Martha insists, "I'd rather believe it makes a difference what I decide to do. For instance . . ."

"It might make a difference, it's just that you can't tell what the difference will turn out to be."

"If you're so interested in what we think, why don't you ever listen to us?"

They walk out on me before I can make amends. One's family can be as unkind as strangers. When I argued the point in print, a reader, Shirley Aronson, wrote to *The Village Voice:* "We no longer live in the deterministic world of Sir Isaac Newton, but we don't yet live in a completely insane and irrational one. Why does Mr. Vizinczey bother writing? If he presses down on his typewriter key, doesn't he expect to see a letter formed as a result of his action?"

There is no doubt whatever that one looks like an utter fool, arguing the futility of expectations.

I write in longhand, however, and would never touch a

typewriter—which just goes to show that even the most matter-of-fact assumption can be pure fantasy. Of course, the more immediate and tangible are the results of our actions, the more reliable our guesses about them are likely to be. But there is never a predetermined connection. The pressed typewriter key does not, I understand, necessarily produce a letter on the page; this betrayal of reasonable expectations keeps the service industry in business. It also accounts for the peculiar poignancy of air crashes. Anyone who takes a plane to some sunny place expects to arrive there, yet many die on the way. Taking even a good guess for certain knowledge is to ignore an often small but always essential gap in the logic of occurrences.

I I

STILL, IF events occur in an irrational way, why does one, or why should one, bother doing anything? There is no answer to this question, just as there is no answer to the question why we go on living. As a means to an end, the act of living would be pointless: the logic of result-oriented thinking is suicide.

But the notion that people are (or ought to be) breathing for the results is so much part of our thinking that we cannot get rid of it simply by realizing its absurdity. Who would consider it worthwhile to take a deep breath of fresh air if it didn't make any difference to his health? Without the benefit of a good reason we are at a loss to make much sense out of what we do. I write this with the memory of a splitting headache, which is giving me a new one, a remnant of my childhood.

I was about fourteen at the time, a shy and grave boy, much taken by my teachers' admonition that we were rational human beings. Everything had to be justified for me: I wouldn't let my legs run away with me unless I was late for school or could join the race to the corner. My brother gave me a good hiding one day because I wanted to know what good he thought it would do to keep combing his hair, once he had combed it. Yet I wasn't criticizing, just curious. I was always pestering people to tell me their reasons, and couldn't understand why nobody was fond of my company. There was one person, however, one of the girls in our class, who *didn't mind* my presence, there was nothing more to it than that—I remember she had a frown and an elegant blue leather schoolbag I very much envied. We often walked homeward from school together, discussing matters. In fact she was a far more accomplished rationalist than I was, for she could help me with my homework in mathematics. I had a very high opinion of her, and one afternoon, the day after my brother had bought me a pair of skis and I was feeling particularly sporty (not having yet broken my leg), I told Katalin that I loved her.

This was on the street, just an impulsive remark, I hadn't really considered the pros and cons of loving her—an omission which I immediately regretted, as Katalin wanted an explanation. I asked her to give me time to think about it, but she wouldn't. She had often suspected me of being in love with her, she said, and I must have had more than enough time to consider my reasons. I said I thought she was pretty, but this she dismissed (and I had to agree with her) as an insufficient explanation, as there were countless girls prettier than she was. But then, why? She thought I was just trying to be difficult.

I brooded over the matter all evening, trying to pinpoint my reasons, so that I could explain them to her the next day. Why should I love Katalin, I asked myself, and, more to the point, *what purpose would it serve?* I disliked her for giving me a headache (it kept me awake half the night) and I decided it was senseless to waste my time thinking about her at all.

I I I

WE ARE confused, we often don't know how to feel, what to do, because we're looking for clues in the wrong place— in the place where there is nothing, neither air nor sunshine, in the place of tomorrow which does not yet exist. The results of our feelings and our actions are unknown to us. We have our expectations, of course, but whether these expectations are to be fulfilled or proven wrong in the unforeseeable future, they are only fantasies at the present. To decide what to do, we ought to try to resist the guidance of our guesses. The only way to cope with reality is to rely on what is real, and there is nothing so real in this world as your own being.

Those who cry "look ahead!" are fools, con men or murderers who want us to stare into a vacuum until we start hallucinating. The true password is "look inside!"

THE DEVIL tempts us to betray our instincts, our desires, our honor, our common sense, by conjuring false mirages of "the consequences." He invented fear and hope to corrupt us.

"Don't climb the tree," he tells the boys who are testing the strength of the lowest branches, "you'll fall down and get hurt. Remember what your mother told you! Restrain yourselves! All you have to do is lower your heads. If you don't look up at the sky, you'll forget about climbing."

If the boys get bored with fear, the Devil works on their hopes. He dissuades them from climbing by promising them more magnificent trees in the next wood: they can climb as high as they please some other time, so long as they do nothing now.

When his victims tire of doing nothing, he leads them to a swamp. "Go ahead," he urges them, "there's a beautiful forest on the other side. Yes, I know this place smells awful and your feet are sinking in the mud, but restrain your senses. Go ahead, go in deeper. And stop holding your noses—you're making an emotional judgment!"

Often the Devil appears in the disguise of an economist.

"You're unhappy because you aren't prosperous enough. Build more factories and highways. You'll see, as soon as the air turns brown we'll all breathe easier!"

"You want peace and quiet?" the Devil asks. "Quick, build runways by your bedroom windows. If jets take off and land in your backyards, you'll be able to fly to silent places!"

When you're obsessed by fear and hope, you're possessed by the Devil.

V

THIS IS a rough prose translation of Attila József's "Epitaph for a Spanish Peasant":

> General Franco drafted me into his army,
> I didn't desert, I was scared he would have me
> shot,
> I was scared—that's why I fought against justice and liberty
> On the walls of Irún. Even so, death reached
> me.

V I

THE PEASANT who didn't want to fight against liberty might have survived fighting against Franco, or in hiding. He might have been shot dead, or he might have survived regardless of what he did. He simply had no "pragmatic," sensible way to make the choice between giving in, fighting back or running away.

But then why not take heart from this uncertain state of affairs? We have no way to avoid suffering and death, but while we are alive we can please ourselves while taking our chances. Whatever our predicament, it is always possible to respond as we would desire to—and still survive.

Yet how often we think, in far less extreme circumstances than a civil war, that we are forced to do the thing we hate!

"I had no choice," claims the opportunist.

"He had no character," comments the moralist.

"He had no imagination," concludes the sage.

V I I

Throughout history, men have built themselves imaginary prisons, where their deepest longings for joy and adventure are barred from fulfillment by the iron gates of "impossibility." The world is full of people whom no one has put in chains but who bind themselves with frozen thoughts and fears.

A man whose mind conforms to the conditioned responses of his daily life is a coward and a slave. To free himself, he must free his imagination, so that he may conceive the world as it is: a place where it is possible to be adventurous, that is, to be himself.

V I I I

We have less control over others and more power over ourselves than we like to think.

I X

Once we understand that we live in an irrational world, we can understand that we are free to act—and ought to act—spontaneously, for we cannot count on any other reward for our action than the satisfaction of doing it.

A man is free when he understands that every act is like the act of love.

THIS IS said to the reader whom I imagine to be sane and decent. As the demented killer has become the central figure of both news and entertainment, people tend to react to such a proposition from the point of view of how it would affect a repressed criminal psychopath, and I've been reprimanded by readers for arguing the wisdom of the hippies' cry "do your own thing!" as a justification of murder, torture, and exploitation.

But isn't the difference between joy and crime apparent to most people—except perhaps to those who believe that we should spend our lives performing duties which make us miserable? As for the man who claims murder as his own thing, he at least has to face up to the truth that he is a murderer by choice. Few people in fact desire the actual horrors they perpetrate: they glory in the future "benefits" of their crimes. ("I did it for my country," said Robert Kennedy's assassin.)

It is quite possible that the attitude which encourages madmen to run amok can keep the rest of us sane; it is possible that self-indulgence is the only sanity drug.

X I

READER, HOW I WISH I could call on the persuasive powers of Stendhal, an egotist worth knowing, to tempt you with your longings!

I write this as a letter, express, special delivery, to remind the recipient that our destiny has no boundaries; I hope it will reach those who feel trapped in their lives, who have lost faith in their freedom.

I know what it is to bend and smile without prompting, yet I still say:

Why be scared? No one can deny us the air we breathe! It is not so easy to be destroyed as we fear; so there is no point in letting ourselves be blackmailed for our insignificance. Whatever happens to us, we still have the royal prerogative to grant ourselves the freedom to be what we want to be. We have nothing to lose but our unhappiness, the misery of denying our own being and dignity. At the most desperate times, I have often been able to rescue my self-respect from the insolence of people on whom my next month's rent depended by telling them, with all due reverence: *fuck off*.

X I I

"You just cannot say that people ought to do only what they really want to do," says my wife. "What about the husband and father who has small children to support? He can't risk his job, however much he hates it. You're glorifying irresponsibility."

Yet what exactly is responsibility, if it rests on the denial of personality? I know a father of five children who used to be the chief engineer of a large public utility. He was gloomy and irritable, fought with his wife, suffered prolonged fits of depression and eventually had a nervous breakdown, which took him to a psychiatrist. After some months of pursuing false leads, they discovered what the man had always known, that he loathed his job, hated electrical engineering and always had, and that the only activity he really enjoyed was gardening. The psychiatrist advised him to give up his job, but for over a year he refused to do so: he couldn't just throw away his professional training, his university degree, his high salary; he had his five children to think of. But as he wasn't getting any better, he took the plunge, left his job and started a small plant nursery on credit. After a few years' hard work he became rich; but having learned that flowers are his lifeline, he sticks to working in his greenhouses.

There may not always be a way where there's a will, but on the other hand—if success isn't certain, neither is failure.

At any rate, the young rightly show no gratitude for the inheritance of a vile world which their fathers maintained by denying their best instincts "for the sake of the children."

X I I I

ONLY THE means can justify the end, or excuse it, whatever that end turns out to be.

The fact that results develop in a haphazard way is the most compelling argument for decency. The uncertainty of good results robs us of the excuses which allow us to commit vicious acts with a clear conscience. There is nothing more "pragmatic" than our instinctive revulsion from violence.

Moreover, those who are concerned with the reality of their means are likely to choose their ends wisely. If our dreams aren't to be fulfilled they should at least be splendid.

X I V

IN A CHAOTIC world, moral decisions are the only rational ones.

X V

MANY EVILS come to pass because people cannot conceive that they could happen; that's how Hitler became chancellor. If there is a nuclear exchange, this ought to be our epitaph: "They are extinct because they lacked imagination."

X V I

THE COROLLARY of *no man controls his future* is *neither does anybody else.* People submit to oppression through a misunderstanding.

Many positive acts of self-assertion—acts for the individual or the common good—are never attempted because people think they couldn't possibly achieve their purpose. Yet, in an irrational universe, it is illogical to suppose that the conditions of exploitation, misery, and ignorance are inevitable and unchangeable.

There is no point in striving for a utopia we can neither build nor maintain in the chaos of perpetual flux. But in a permanently changing world, evil ought to be and can be permanently resisted.

The Greatness of Eugene McCarthy

Les grandes âmes ne sont pas soupçonnées, elles se cachent, ordinairement il ne paraît qu'un peu d'originalité. Il y a plus de grandes âmes qu'on ne le croirait.

Stendhal: *De l'Amour*

I'M WRITING about a living man and I do not know whether he will be forgotten in four years' time or whether, on the contrary, he will be far better known to the distant reader than he is to me. And even if he were to be known, what in the end would he be known for? A man's courage is no more certain than his fame. But no one understands this better than Eugene McCarthy: he has too much pride to play the hero or to prostrate himself before the oracle at Delphi begging for undecipherable predictions. Such are the secrets of great souls.

I write of an American, even a great American, with some reluctance. Empires advance not only by land, sea, and air—they occupy the airwaves, the television screens, the pages of newspapers and books, blotting out the rest of the world. They spread over the imagination of mankind, malignantly, for they distort our sense of our own dimensions. It is as if the whole world were America, Russia, and China, with a few odd, small tribes here and there, not worthy of much attention. Far more people died in Biafra than in Vietnam, but as the Biafrans did not have the good fortune to be starved and massacred by an imperial army, their tragedy aroused less sympathy and indignation—even in England, although much of the killing was done by the small arms of the British government. More Britons despised Harold Wilson for his verbal support of President Johnson than for his silent peddling of guns and armored cars to suppress a small African nation. Americans often complain about such instances of a double standard; but if they are judged more harshly, it's not because they are seen as worse or better than other people—it's just because they seem more *real*.

They are more *important*, the reader may oblige me by thinking, manifesting the attitude I'm trying to describe. For how are we to measure importance if not in human terms, in the number of dead and dying? In what sense could the British government be less important than the American, during the days when it was helping to kill more people? The metaphysical dimension of intrinsic significance that we attribute to the crimes and glories of great nations has nothing to do with the world—it has to do with our enslaved imagination, with our unequal awareness of the indivisible reality of all human experience.

I'm a beneficiary of this malady, so I may decry it without hesitation. I started out in life as a Hungarian, then became a Canadian, and am now a Londoner; I write in English; yet publishers everywhere claim that they have translated my novel "from the American." There's more money in it that way. The very same novel, even if it's all in Japanese, would obviously attract less attention if it had been translated from mere English or Albanian. As if the value, interest, and importance of a book *or any other human act* could lie anywhere but in the act itself!

Now read this carefully: the son of a small nation, writing in the capital of a former empire, I declare that every spot on earth is equally precious, that the importance of every emotion, every thought, word, and deed lies in its own beauty or ugliness, in its own truth or falsehood.

I say *declare* and I call on seven continents to pay attention to a spot as central as any other on this round globe. My South Kensington flat no less than a Japanese teahouse, the kitchen of a whorehouse in Naples, the marketplace in Lusaka, a guerrilla hideout in Bolivia or the steps of the White House—they are all equally legitimate forums from which to address mankind. And no one can tell the importance of what is being said by the direction the words are drifting from. You have no choice but to listen to them all, difficult as it is. If you are at least aware that men become *important* only through what they create from their own flesh and blood, for good or ill, then you may perceive your own significance, the meaning of your own life, the value of your own soul.

So I'm writing about Eugene McCarthy, not on account of his being an American politician, but hoping that I can persuade even my American readers to look at him as they would look at Alexander Dubcek of Czechoslovakia, or at someone who wasn't a politician at all—as a man attempting to live with his conscience. For however much Americans may have in common as Americans, they have more in common as human beings. Indeed, there is no better way to understand one's own brother than to forget that he is a relative and see him as a man. It may be, in fact, that Americans have become so violently opposed to one another because of the delusion that the bond that ties them together is American history and tradition rather than the flesh which they have in common with all mankind. There is something in this, even if it isn't the whole story.

What is American about Eugene McCarthy (a difference which may disappear in time) is that he is better known than the great men of Finland. And if I speak of him, it isn't to make you forget about your neighbors but rather to remind you of them through a man who has shown that greatness comes as naturally to nobodies as to anybody else—there are more great men in the world than one would suspect. Certainly no one suspected Eugene McCarthy.

McCarthy was one of the few members of the U.S. Senate who hadn't got rich representing the people, but apart from this sign of some originality, he was plodding through life like any unremarkable middle-class pro in the world, an obscure politician living from term to term, mixing good intentions and compromises, getting along but not getting anywhere—a politician who had passed his prime without acquiring any powerful backers or sizable following—who wrote poetry in secret and had no prospects. These days, though, my stepdaughters here in London often quote his famous lines:

> Stubbornness and penicillin hold
> the aged above me.

The poetry isn't without inspiration; and as for his un-distinguished career, what could be more inspiring? We tend to think that we are defined by our past, that we cannot do better than our yesterdays; McCarthy has shown that it is never too late to create one's valor.

At the age of fifty-two he suddenly found the courage to commit political suicide by choosing to run for the job of leading his nation—and to run against his own party's President-in-office, who could not possibly be denied the nomination and seemed assured of reelection. Moreover, he based his candidacy on a single issue, the Vietnam war, which according to the polls had the support of the majority of the electorate. In America that kind of thing is not thought to recommend a professional politician for further office. In any case, President Johnson, a man with a mean memory, with not only the machinery of the state and the party but also the power of public opinion at his command, would know how to put such a renegade out of a job for good. Heightening the hilarity of the brave comedy, this self-styled candidate who had *nothing going for him*, as the saying goes, no organization, no campaign funds, no campaigners and no name for himself, went to battle against the Chief Executive in the New Hampshire primary, a mock election too inconsequential for the President to contest in person. The only prize had to do with conscience, his own and his countrymen's: he could force the American electorate (presumed to be either apathetic, indifferent or positively in favor of the carnage in Vietnam) to declare their feelings about the war at the polls.

In an age when men are often obliged to affirm their integrity by facing firing squads or going to prison, it is easy to overlook the full measure of his heroism. In truth, the ultimate sacrifices of life and liberty distort our own moral dilemmas: we tend to make our small evil compromises in the proud knowledge that we could die for a great cause if need be. The risks Eugene McCarthy took were more prosaic. He exposed himself to the two things a man is least willing to face—losing his livelihood and looking like a fool.

To everyone's surprise, including his own, McCarthy won the New Hampshire primary and President Johnson announced his decision to retire from politics. The response McCarthy evoked in New Hampshire and beyond, far beyond the borders of the United States itself, had to do with more than revulsion from the Vietnam war. It had to do primarily with McCarthy's "hopeless stand," which showed that it is possible for us to free ourselves from the frustrating tyranny of tomorrow, from the imagined obligation to avoid failures even at the expense of our souls. He gave flesh to the notion that it is more fun to do the right thing than to live in apathy or worry about success. "A politician without ambition," as McCarthy once said of himself, "is a dangerous animal."

To be great is to assume great concerns.

Yet the world is willing to grant great concerns only to the powerful. At the time of Robert Kennedy's murder, the newspapers were filled with tributes to his compassion for the dispossessed, his often expressed and undoubtedly genuine desire to help the Negroes, the migrant workers and other exploited minorities. Without wishing to detract from the humanity of the Kennedy prince or any other generous-hearted aristocrat, one still must find something offensive in the presumption that it is natural for the eminent to concern themselves with the world, while the rest of us are expected to be absorbed in our own little lives. The students in particular are arousing a great deal of indignation by engaging in protest and political action instead of sticking to their desks. If you have ever worried about the state of the world and tried to do something about it, you must be equally familiar with the spoken or unspoken questions: why do you feel so strongly about it? what makes you think it's any of your business?

In a more polite way, such comments were made about Eugene McCarthy: an obscure senator presuming to take upon himself the conscience of America, a virtual nobody assuming the responsibilities of greatness. Between the lines one could hear the cry: Who does he think he is?

And of course it is the nobodies who ask such questions first—for a man remains a nobody by accepting the role, by drawing himself the line: I shall go this far and no farther. So McCarthy knew his place; he would not dream of running for president. He waited for the heir apparent to come forward, the man who had the best chance, the man of whom such great history-making actions were expected. Of himself, he expected no more than to go finally to Robert Kennedy, to ask him to declare his candidacy. But the heir apparent declined McCarthy's request: it didn't look like a winning proposition to run against President Johnson, not even for a Kennedy.

Robert Kennedy was a *pragmatist*. He would rather deny himself the satisfaction of having a go at Lyndon Johnson, whom he detested, than risk spoiling his chances

for the presidency in 1972. He was *sensible* and *realistic*—
he was sick with the sickness of the century. He was blind
to mortality; it was excluded from his moral and political
considerations. Haunted by the violent deaths of two
brothers and a sister, convinced that he too would die
young, carelessly risking his life on many occasions, he still
thought it made good sense for him to sacrifice 1968 for
1972. He was an efficient and busy man who never wasted
a minute, never had time to reflect upon his own being, and
so remained fundamentally stupid. If he had given himself
time to relax and think, he might at least have considered
the threats to his own life in relation to the problem of how
he should spend it. It might then have occurred to him that
he had no right to postpone his concerns, his causes, his
ambition, or even his spite—that in truth no man had the
right to postpone himself, as it were. Perhaps then he
would have been ready to declare his candidacy when the
older man asked him to.

McCarthy could not have foreseen that Robert Kennedy's life would soon be ended, but it must have struck
him as strange that anyone, let alone a Kennedy, could be
more worried about the 1972 election, over four years
away, than about the choice that had to be made at the
moment. He himself, past fifty and still a backbench legis-
lator, must by then have become sceptical about his own
future (and the reader ought to note this, if he is to grasp
how a nobody can grow into a great man); but it may have
been while listening to Kennedy's plans for 1972 that he
finally understood, not only with his mind but in his bones,
how obscenely irrational it was to try to win tomorrow's
games. Was it the temporizing heir apparent's anxiety
about the kingdom he might lose that made McCarthy

realize his own strength, the strength of the commoner for whom the next day held only dangers and no promises? After the meeting with Robert Kennedy, while everybody was weighing the results of events that might never happen, the desire must have grown in McCarthy to *create his present*, to assert his conscience against his country's course of monstrous crimes and ignoble defeats.

Pondering the impossibilities of politics, he must have understood that a man is free to choose only what meaning he gives to his life, that he cannot *secure* any other victory.

The man who understood this was no longer a cog in the machine. In a country going mad with the notion that there was no limit to what human beings (and especially Americans) could achieve, he stepped forward to demonstrate the only valid response to the chaos of life: *do your own thing.*

With his candidacy he expressed the wisdom of the hippie cry in the context of the great moral dilemma which was tearing apart his country, and it suddenly made sense to millions.

It was a liberation from despair, if only for a time. These are the days of righteous violence, when just grievances are avenged on innocent bystanders and maiming and murder appear to be the only viable forms of communication. "To show you what I mean, I'm obliged to kill you," is the way the talk goes just now. Housewives and Negro militants are buying guns in America to debate the problem of the slums, and municipal police are turning into combat troops to fight the dispossessed and the young; the war of the races and the war of the generations are being prepared to secure the victory of desolation and death. Yet these are also the days of the malaise of helplessness, when most of us suffer paralysis of the will in face of a world hurtling on to new horrors and ever more visible chaos, impervious to our attempts to improve it or hold it together. What should we do—act or fold our arms? The sphere of action becomes increasingly violent, while quiescence is a form of self-immolation. The void at the center of the whirlpool swallows those who give up.

Enjoying his fruitless fight, McCarthy conveyed the best of two thousand years of philosophy: the suggestion that the violence and the apathy of our present impasse grow from looking at our predicament upside-down; that we ask the wrong question when we ask how we should manage the world, instead of how we should assert ourselves in the world. What mattered wasn't whether McCarthy could end the war, but that he rejected it. The war was beyond his power; its resolution was up to chance, but his rejection of it was up to him.

Accepting the limits of the human condition, less worried about the consequences than the challenge, he affirmed the serenity of good conscience. It had great appeal. For while we think we can be moved to action only by the prospect of achieving some purpose, fulfilling some plan, in truth we act because it is our nature to do so. Nature has no justification and needs none. The result of life is death, yet we go on living. So McCarthy went on campaigning.

The lack of such indulgence has caused the greatest horrors of our times. Allowing our actions to be dictated by future ends, however noble, we abandon the real world for fantasies. Would the saturation bombing of Dresden have been possible, could the A-bomb have fallen on Hiroshima, would the splinter bombs have disemboweled Vietnamese children, if these horrors had been considered as actions *for their own sake, on their own merits?* Only the results count, we say, and we hardly notice when we bloody our hands.

Not so, said McCarthy, only what we do matters—as for the rest, why speculate? He showed us how we could attain, if not peace, at least our peace of mind.

Still, what was the use!

I would not have felt compelled to argue the futility of expectations and the madness of presuming to know the future if I were not exorcising my greatest personal failing, and contrary to every proposition in this book, I could not help feeling certain that Eugene McCarthy would be the next President of the United States. I even had bets on it. More: when I planned *The Rules of Chaos*, I intended to call on McCarthy's victory at the Democratic Convention and on his election to the presidency to prove that hopeless causes are not always quite as pointless as they seem.

For it is one thing to lecture wisdom to one's family or be cool and clever on paper, and quite another to be able to continue thinking uninfluenced by one's sympathies and hopes.

McCarthy, too, had begun to hope and once he succumbed to the temptation of *thinking ahead*, creating the only shameful episode of his campaign. Envisaging the destructive impact of Russia's invasion of Czechoslovakia on his own country's chances of democratization (a fact that ought to have reminded him of the indivisible misery of humanity), he refused to be moved by the tragedy of another nation, by the tragedy of politicians who were not unlike himself in their efforts to salvage their country without violence. He said that, learning the news at midnight, he would have gone to bed. Yet greatness, too, is the grace of the day, and many people around the world did not go to bed when McCarthy was eliminated from the presidential race.

The papers referred to his campaign with disappointed condescension, like so many girls who were nasty to the handsome young man but didn't mean him to go away (either Humphrey or McCarthy would do, *The New York Times* had editorialized at the opening of the Chicago convention—soon they were editorializing about George Wallace). And it is still fashionable in America to refer to McCarthy's heroic attempt as an interesting failure which didn't make any difference one way or the other. Nonetheless, even his defeat proved that McCarthy was right, that what mattered was the campaign, not the victory. As President McCarthy would not have inherited any more divine power than his predecessors, it is impossible to say what he could have achieved beyond a speedy disengagement from Southeast Asia. But it is easy to see what disasters his *absence* has been causing.

While there was a man in the public eye who had the courage to make sacrifices without the certitudes which would have allowed him to sacrifice others, whose moral passion was strong enough to move him to act but not to shout, who would rather laugh than shake his fist—then everything was possible, even brotherhood and order.

From the film *Easy Rider* (COLUMBIA PICTURES INDUSTRIES, INC.)

Rule Number Four
DELUSIONS KILL

I

In recent history, it seems, only policemen have taken ideas seriously. Who in the United States could match J. Edgar Hoover's *concern* for what people are thinking? University faculties, cultural foundations and learned societies certainly haven't shown anything like the same excitement about the whole corpus of Western philosophy as Mr. Hoover has been able to work up about communist-anarchist leaflets—only to be floored, at the end of a lifetime of ceaseless labor, by the discovery that America is being overrun by hordes of mystics.

Conflicts of belief (the sort of things that interest policemen) are even less real than direct military confrontations: we are defeated not by creeping enemy ideologies but by the haphazard interrelationship of ideas and events.

II

As a rule, the most dangerous ideas are not the ones that divide people but those on which they agree.

III

Most people picture civilization as a mountain with the twentieth century near the summit and think that they can see far and wide by virtue of their position. The young, of course, who grasp at first sight that their ancestors haven't grown brighter since they came down from the trees, can comment on the square notion of intellectual progress in no uncertain terms; yet they seem convinced that by virtue of this insight they have become wiser than their elders—which is to say that they have joined those who believe in the progress of enlightenment.

Martha and Mary, as I've already complained, have no doubt that they're smarter than their mother or myself—lively limbs generate an incredible amount of intellectual pride. And, of course, all of us living assume that we know more than the dead whose brains have already been devoured by worms. People flock around the sorcerer, the priest, the scientist, the commissar, the psychiatrist, the drug pusher, each generation of the faithful pitying the victims of past fallacies, and this repetitive vanity keeps us stupider than we need to be.

I V

ONE OF THE cruder expressions of this vanity is the notion that people grow wiser by becoming better informed.

"I've spent thousands of wonderful hours learning facts," recalls a ruined Chicago businessman wistfully, musing on the shambles of his life. (I'm quoting from Studs Terkel's collection of interviews, *Division Street: America.*) Facts have become mental drugs which soothe the pain of bewilderment and induce in the addict's mind colorful visions of himself as an intelligent being coming to grips with reality. As our technological civilization becomes ever more chaotic, there is a dramatic increase in fact-taking and in fact production—itself a compensatory activity of specialists struggling to overcome their own sense of the Absurd.

Computers are the chief depositories of this poisonous substance, "data," which paralyzes our nerve centers and numbs our sense of infinity, so that we no longer know that millions and billions of facts relate in the same way to reality as a single punch card of information, making us in no way wiser.

V

IT SEEMS THAT we can learn something only at the price of forgetting something else. Scientific knowledge, for instance, has developed along with a corresponding increase in ignorance about the vengefulness of nature. Primitive man worshiped the river, believing it to be a god, but for all his superstitious ignorance he wasn't such a great fool as to arouse his river's anger by poisoning it.

V I

BACK IN THE OLD DAYS when science was still taken very seriously, even by the young, I wrote a play called *The Bomber*, about a research biochemist, Guy Foster, who goes berserk when he loses his faith in science and acts upon the proposition that "fire isn't necessarily destructive, it creates open space." (He lives in New York.) This agnostic fantasy, printed in 1962, brought me abusive letters from such remote citadels of darkness as the Massachusetts Institute of Technology, particularly about the scene in Guy Foster's experimental laboratory where cats are dissected; so the problem may still be of some nostalgic interest to those over thirty.

> (an improbable) WORKMAN: The way I see it, it's got so you just say the word "reason" and people lose their heads altogether. Not me, thanks. Old-fashioned common sense is good enough for me.
>
> FOSTER: So you don't think science does any good?
>
> WORKMAN: A lot of good, sure—but you can say that much for the devil himself.
>
> FOSTER: . . . You think you'd rather live in the Middle Ages?
>
> WORKMAN: Since you ask me—I think maybe I would. The Inquisition didn't have a stake that could burn the whole human race. And Doctor, you can't deny there's more beauty in cathedrals than in laboratories. Besides, with the money you spend you could be feeding the world.
>
> FOSTER: You talk glibly, but it isn't that simple—great minds could go mad on these contradictions.
>
> WORKMAN: That's just what I mean. You put it much better than I could. They go mad.
>
> FOSTER: (to his assistant) Could you tell this fellow anything he hasn't got an answer for?
>
> ASSISTANT: We've fired him.

V I I

To MARY AND MARTHA and their boy friends all this is pathetically out of date. The time when poor old bishops and scientists will cry on each other's shoulders for lack of young people ready to devote themselves to the Faith doesn't appear to be too far off.

At any rate, Mary was eleven when she decided to stop paying attention to her science courses, although she finds biology amusing. It is through *involvement* and *awareness* that she will reach her Nirvana.

I wonder whether I'm being a spoilsport, arguing for the inclusion of understanding.

Awareness is a condition of bewilderment and anxiety that propels either toward understanding or (more often) toward self-deception and delusion. Primitive man, exposed to the elements, could not have been more aware of or involved in the storm (he saw it, he heard it, he smelled it, he felt it, he experienced it in every possible way) but he did not know what it was all about. So he thought the thunder and lightning were the revenge of the spirits, and if his tribe decided that he was the one who had roused the divine anger, he got killed. The difference between understanding and awareness is the difference between cooperation and murder, between life and death.

V I I I

WHAT THE CAVEMAN didn't know about the storm didn't hurt him; it was what he *assumed* he knew that caused his tragedy.

When we reflect upon past horrors like witch burning, the sort of crimes which were held up to us in school as proof that scientific knowledge had advanced human wisdom, we find that these cruelties sprang not from men's lack of knowledge but from their readiness to believe and act upon their fantasies.

What is wrong with modern man's faith in science is what was wrong with the caveman's faith in his mumbo jumbo or the inquisitor's faith in his theology—the presumption that he finally knows enough to fix the future by wrecking the present. We still fail to understand that, the possible occurrences being infinite, everything we know is of relative validity, for its exact significance (relevance or irrelevance) depends on all that we do *not* know and all that we *cannot* know—i.e., the future. We consider scientific truths so absolute that we do not mind our governments spending the nations' fortunes on them, even though these infallible truths are continually being modified or canceled out by further discoveries or new combinations of events. Scientists themselves are well aware that their discoveries are conditional; yet with the insincerity of the agnostic popes and bishops of an earlier religion, most of them continue to propagate the fraud that the observations and insights of Copernicus, Newton and Einstein belong to a different order of exactitude and universality than Shakespeare's observations and insights about jealousy in *Othello*—while in fact each truth is of limited relevance (to what degree we cannot tell) and for precisely the same reason: because of the infinite number of ways in which everything could interrelate in the future.

The failure to appreciate this led people to consider *safe* atomic fallout, cigarettes, cancerous soft drinks, food poisoned by chemicals, birth control pills, Thalidomide—why, people would take up the bubonic plague if only enough scientific authorities would approve it.

More than any other body of human knowledge, science is necessarily founded (as Whitehead put it without my hostile emphasis) on "the concept of an *ideally isolated system*," striving to discover the logic of phenomena without reference to their "*casual contingent dependence* upon detailed items within the rest of the universe," which cannot be examined. But the mythology of science thickens the atmosphere of superstition which encourages us to believe that whenever we catch a glimpse of chaos from another point of view, we become better equipped to control it, and so we still people the invisible regions with all-powerful spirits which demand human sacrifice.

I X

ONE CANNOT SPEAK ill of science without abusing reason, which has been exalted beyond its merits at the expense of our emotions.

Our senses and sensibilities relate us to the present; our reason is an instrument of speculation based on assumptions. Which is why our spontaneous inclinations, our "emotional judgments" are usually more correct than our calculated decisions—reason forever leads us astray.

The crimes of reason—the crimes of assumption—have always exceeded the crimes of passion. Animal experts (in great fashion among intellectuals) claim that the world is a bloody mess because of our violent nature, but I would argue that apes and coral fish are not such useful clues to human nature as man's own history. And history suggests that if people would torture, maim, and kill only when driven by a genuine desire to do so, the world would not be free of violence, but it would be unimaginably peaceful.

It isn't our emotions that we need to keep under control, but our reason. Restrain yourselves, restrain your reasonings!

APART FROM atavistic urges to aggression and destruction (less frequent than we like to pretend these days), our emotions tend to turn murderous and suicidal when they are perverted by reason. For instance, there is nothing wrong with fear, one of our survival instincts. It is when we reason ourselves toward some ideal of heroism which excludes fear that we become dangerous fools. "In a military retreat," wrote Stendhal, "if you warn an Italian soldier of some danger ahead which it is useless to confront, he will thank you and take pains to avoid it. Give the same well-intentioned warning to a French soldier and he thinks you are challenging him—he is *put on his mettle* and rushes off at once to expose himself to the peril."

It is when we refuse to acknowledge our feelings that we run amok with the mad passion of our rationalizations. Our most malevolent inspirations are shame and guilt, and these are invented by reason to spur us on to further falsifications. But reason is silent about its own villainies.

X I

THIS OBSERVATION is borrowed from a letter which I received. "I agree with your idea that disowned feelings are the worst," the writer said. "When I was a kid, I used to detest the captain of our football team. He was a great player and got straight A's, and everything he did filled me with disgust. Once I saw him picking his nose—I couldn't pick my own for weeks afterward. But now that I don't mind being envious, I can be fond of people I envy. After all, they've got something I appreciate."

X I I

NO LEARNING or reasoning can substitute for intelligence, which is a sense of what is real: a sense of one's own being and the world.

The wise are those who aren't afraid to imagine what exists, who are not so vain as to deny what they feel, who have the courage to reflect upon what they experience—and who have too much pride to take refuge in fantasies.

X I I I

OUR MOST dangerous emotion isn't a thirst for blood but such a seemingly innocent feeling as the desire to feel safe, to be reassured. Ever since the time of Herod, grown men have been massacring children, not out of cruelty but in order to feel more secure.

As the chaotic world can offer us anything except safety, our longing for security is a longing for incomprehension—the inspiration for every kind of delusion and mad behavior.

X I V

CULTURAL HISTORY suggests that men have always had a greater inclination to close their eyes than to open them, to believe comforting lies rather than disconcerting truths.

As we persist in trying to reassure ourselves that we are what we are not, we shun mirrors and seek in the world the affirmation of our self-image: we cherish those ideas, legends, philosophies, sciences, works of art or pseudo-art which confirm our illusions and help us to lie to ourselves. Indeed, it is almost possible to define civilization as man's self-flattery, the dream world which nurtures the existence of the dream person. (P.S. "Too negative to be profound," complained an English critic of this book.)

X V

A PAINFUL TRUTH that civilizations conspire to deny or minimize is the inequality of our good luck.

A man's survival and happiness depend on his existential virtues: his energy, his senses, his mental and emotional capacities, the quality of his intelligence and imagination and physique. In brief, a man depends on his *vitality*. This accident of birth and early childhood imposes itself on maturity and is difficult to improve on in later life; therefore we deny its importance. Western civilization sanctifies the pretense that the feeling and the unfeeling, the strong and the weak, the bright and the stupid, the brave and the cowardly, the charming and the repellent have equal chances in life.

This Great White Lie is asserted by valuing feelings over actions, by rating virtues above ability and intentions above performance.

In religious societies, going to mass on Sunday is considered more virtuous than composing a great mass, because even the tone-deaf can go to church. Similarly, much of the old morality seems to have been inspired by the desire to compensate the sexually weak and deprived by assuring them that they were better than those with strong sex drives and abundant opportunities—while the new ethic of promiscuity assures the emotionally crippled that there is no more to passion than going to bed.

One needs talents and energies and one needs to cultivate them to be a good man, but even the spiteful and the slothful can be upright citizens—can conform, that is, to some standard of good behavior. To be wise one needs intelligence, sensibility, bravery, and a talent for logic, continuously exercised; but the fearfully stupid, too, can have degrees, belong to the most progressive school of thought and assume the most enlightened attitudes.

As far as civilization attempts to justify these pretenses, it is antilife, for it encourages us in our deadening excuses instead of inspiring us to cultivate our abilities, which alone can ensure our survival and happiness.

X V I

To REFLECT upon the delusions of civilization cannot, of course, serve any other useful purpose than to help us to detect our own delusions which we acquired unawares in school and from books, magazines, television or while necking at the movies. There is nothing any of us could possibly do about the chaotic mental condition of mankind; so the only point about other people's false assumptions is what they can teach us about our own.

Indeed, the ability to learn from the follies of others to recognize one's own is another vital element of intelligence. Without this ability one cannot hope to become even as bright as one's capacities would otherwise allow. The difficulty is that most of us tend to assume that seeing through someone else's stupidity is proof of our own wisdom.

X V I I

Two MEN were listening to a fool.

"What a fool you are!" sneered one of the listeners.

"I'm learning from you fools what a fool I am," said the sage gratefully.

X V I I I

WHAT OTHERS THINK may harm or even kill you, depending on chance. Your own delusions, however, are almost certain to be suicidal.

X I X

A MAN'S HEAD is a chaotic place, where reasonings and emotions interact in a haphazard manner, and he is constantly torn between his desire to understand and his desire to be reassured. He is tempted to fill voids with delusions, matching his incapacities with corresponding vanities and his fears with tranquilizing self-deceptions, stupefying himself with rationalizations. So he needs to reflect on his own thoughts with some scepticism and has to be quick to see through his own lies.

In the final analysis, what matters most is not what a man thinks but how he thinks, and how long he is willing to keep it up.

LITERARY DETOUR

WHATEVER a human being does, he expresses not only himself but also his society—a cannibal, for instance, demonstrates with his eating habits both his own character and the spirit of his community. It is in the same way that artists, whether good or bad, document with their works not only their own perceptions but also the mental conditions of the time. This is most self-evident in literature, which consists of nothing but words, the stuff of human consciousness.

A novel may not reveal any truth about life, but it always reveals a great deal about the way we see the world.

From the literary evidence, it appears that violent social changes, by multiplying and intensifying anxieties, drive people to lie to themselves with even greater ingenuity than in periods of relative stability. In times such as ours, rationalizations can grow to the magnitude of psychoses. William Styron's novel *The Confessions of Nat Turner* is a case in point, and it can teach us a great deal about our own temptations to abandon common sense.

On the other hand, when chaos comes to the surface of history, it creates at least the *possibility* that we may perceive the world as it is. If lies grow bigger than ever, they date faster than ever; events shift appearances too quickly to allow them to support any rationalization for too long. It is difficult to keep up one's faith in assumptions when they are being continually and dramatically proved wrong. As we cannot assume anything for long, we have a chance to see things as they are. As the existence of Stendhal's *oeuvre* shows, a chaotic period such as his or ours provides one of history's greatest opportunities for wisdom.

The two following literary arguments are intended to restate the main ideas of this book (as far as possible and with the help of the two novelists' works) in terms of individual consciousness.

Anatomy of Serious Rubbish

or

The Bay of Pigs of the American Literary Establishment

On 27 April 1968 *The Times* reported that New York's City Hall had approved a plan to build a sewage treatment plant in Harlem, against the protests of the only Negro member of the Board of Estimate, who said: "These are the things that make people feel they are not equal . . . you do not understand what you are doing to Harlem." This decision by a liberal city administration (in the wake of the assassination of Martin Luther King, nationwide riots and its own efforts to improve conditions in the ghettos) epitomizes the race problem in America. Most whites are worried about Black Power, they are both afraid and sympathetic, and they wish to improve the Negroes' lot as quickly as possible, but if in the meantime a sewage treatment plant needs to be built, it must be put into Harlem. If something goes wrong, the shit will stink, and white noses must be protected.

So it's not altogether surprising that the most popular and most highly acclaimed novel of that same season in America, the winner of the Pulitzer Prize for fiction in 1968, was William Styron's *The Confessions of Nat Turner*—a compendium of all the rationalizations which prevent white Americans from understanding what they are doing to the blacks and the retribution they are courting.

Styron raises the issue of white oppression and black rebellion in what would appear to be its starkest context, by going back to the days of slavery in his native state of Virginia and evoking one of the bloodiest slave uprisings in American history, the Southampton Insurrection of 1831. Moreover, he has committed himself to a narrative device which promises the harshest possible treatment of his theme, as it seems to preclude any expression of the "prowhite" point of view: the entire work consists of the deathcell meditations of Nat Turner, the rebel leader.

A gifted mechanic and literate lay preacher, history's Turner, like Styron's, set out with only six followers on the night of 21 August 1831 to raise an armed rebellion and free the slaves in Southampton County, in the Tidewater region of southeastern Virginia. For two nights and days they raided the farmhouses on their route, recruiting slaves, capturing horses and weapons and murdering the masters with their families, until they were routed by a body of militia only a few miles from their objective, the armory in the county seat of Jerusalem. Turner escaped and hid in a cave until the end of October, but his sixty-some followers were killed on the spot or executed after summary trials, and as many other blacks were cut down in indiscriminate reprisals; the rebels themselves had butchered fifty-seven white men, women, and children.

However, history's Turner, unlike Styron's, set a time limit to the killing. According to the editor of the Richmond *Enquirer*, who interviewed the leader of the defeated rebels, "indiscriminate slaughter was not their intention after they obtained foothold . . ."; and in his own *Confessions* Turner declared, "*Until we had armed and equipped ourselves and gathered sufficient force*, neither age nor sex was to be spared" (my italics). As he proudly accepted responsibility for the bloodshed and refused to consider himself guilty for what he felt had to be done, there is no reason to doubt his word. These statements and the fact that he did spare a family of poor whites indicate that he rose against the slave-owning class rather than the white race, believing himself appointed by God to slay the serpent of slavery and to lead his people, like Moses, in a crusade against bondage. An impressive character by any standards—but not impressive enough for the novelist, who makes his hero appear even more formidable by turning him into both a religious and racist fanatic who claims "a divine mission to kill all the white people of Southampton and as far beyond as destiny might take me."

For the sake of comparison, I'd like to quote first a slave master's blunt description of his class (in a letter to the editor, published in the Richmond *Whig*):

This is one thing we wish to be understood and remembered—that the Constitution of this State has made Tom, Dick and Harry *property*—it has made Polly, Nancy and Molly *property;* and be that property an evil, a curse or what not, we intend to hold it. Property, which is considered the most valuable by the owners of it, is a nice thing; and for the right thereto to be called in question by an unphilosophical set of political mountebanks, under the influence of supernatural agency or deceit, is insufferable.

Now this is the way Styron's Nat Turner describes the slave masters he has known:

> They ranged down from the saintly . . . to the all right . . . to the barely tolerable . . . to a few who were unconditionally monstrous.

I imagine that William Styron, speaking for himself, would hesitate to describe the morality of any member of the slave-owning class as "all right" or "tolerable"; but the notion of a black racist fanatic (a man who wishes to exterminate not only the slave masters but the entire white race) calling a slave master *saintly* passes beyond the realm of the preposterous into a kind of psychotic credibility. This is the strength of the novel: it confirms white delusions by locating them in the most unlikely and unsuspected source, the mind of Nat Turner.

Although the novel is Nat Turner's stream of consciousness, its flow is determined by T. R. Gray, the court's lawyer. Gray has been haranguing the prisoner and the court with his vicious, stupid opinions about blacks in general and uppity niggers in particular, and Turner responds to these ravings (which he remembers word for word) by recalling his life as a slave and a rebel in such a way as to prove Gray's every point. What Gray gloated and jeered at, Turner sadly deplores; the calumnies are made to stick with pity and regret.

The most important of these naturally concerns the threat implied by the revolt of the blacks, a threat which Gray disposes of at the beginning and keeps disposing of throughout the novel. This is part of his address to the court, as Turner remembers it:

> ". . . the defendant's confessions, paradoxically, far from having to alarm us, from sending us into consternation and confusion, should instead give us considerable cause for relief. . . . all such rebellions are not only likely to be exceedingly rare in occurrence but are ultimately doomed to failure, and this as a result of the basic weakness and inferiority, the moral deficiency of the Negro character."

And this is how Turner reacts:

> Now as Gray spoke, the same sense of misery and despair I had felt that first day when, in the cell, Gray had tolled off the list of slaves acquitted, transported, but not hung—*them other niggers, dragooned, balked, it was them other niggers that cooked your goose, Reverend*—this same despair suddenly rolled over me in a cold and sickening wave . . .

(*125*)

Far from disagreeing with the general proposition, Styron's Turner brings up a particular instance to support it (another significant invention—there is no historical evidence that unwilling slaves were forced to join the rebellion, much less that they "balked" and brought about its defeat).

Nat Turner, who remembers so much, doesn't happen to recall any detail which would effectively contradict Gray's assertion that the oppressors should feel all the more secure on account of his exceedingly rare rebellion; but he is profuse with recollected examples of Negro docility, even confirming as a fact of his experience the myth that Negroes never commit suicide:

> . . . I had to admit to myself, as I thought more deeply about it, that I had never known of a Negro who had killed himself; and in trying to explain this fact, I tended to believe . . . that [it was the Negro's] will toward patience and forbearance in the knowledge of life everlasting, which swerved him away from the idea of self-destruction.

It's the sweet note of flattery that makes the lie so nauseating. To say that Negroes are docile would be too crude, but to *admire* them for being more patient and forbearing than other members of the human race is spicing the joys of prejudice with magnanimity.

As a matter of fact, the slaves were no more forbearing than you or I: the slavocracy could maintain its power only by the continuous marching of troops and citizens' patrols and by beating to death and hanging not only suspected or real slave rebels, but also their white helpers. Even so, Turner's revolt was only one episode in a long history of plots, escapes, fires, murders, assaults and guerrilla sorties of runaway slaves, which made the South about as safe for Americans as Saigon is today.

The best guide to the period is Herbert Aptheker's fascinating study *American Negro Slave Revolts*, the book to turn to if you're interested in the facts. Here facts are relevant only so far as they indicate the force of rationalizations. Despite his twenty years' research into the historical background, Styron was able to conceive a Nat Turner who had absolutely no inkling of the brave attempts of other Negroes and not the slightest hope that there would ever be another rebel to take his place. Which is inexplicable until we remember one of the basic laws of self-deception: we regard all events which contradict our hopes as exceptions to the rule and therefore as of no significance.

Still, this alone would not have been enough, for even if one ignores the historical record, it is self-evident that it is impossible to force millions of human beings to live like animals without permanent trouble and fear of trouble. Styron and his liberal admirers could have blinded themselves to this elementary fact of social psychology only by believing that the Negroes don't belong to the same human race as the rest of us, that they're not subject to the same basic responses as we are—which is indeed how those in power have always viewed the oppressed, and not only those of another color. Stalin's best Hungarian pupil, the dictator Rákosi, made jokes about the sheeplike nature of his countrymen right up to the second day of the 1956 revolution, when he caught a plane out of the country only minutes before the rebels took over the airport.

In the society of the family, as long as men denied all rights to their wives, daughters, and sisters, they were convinced that women were naturally and contentedly sub-missive.

To free ourselves from guilt and the fear of retribution, we have always been quick to invent inherent and irre-mediable deficiencies for the people we persecute, who can thus be seen as *Nature*'s victims.

But while the oppressed are despised for their meekness, they are continually advised that it would be both immoral and useless for them to act like men and hit back. So Styron's lawyer, Gray, never tires of reminding the chained prisoner (whose only remaining chance of violence is to kick violently on the gallows) that his rebellion was absolutely futile and, worse, only increased the slaves' suffering.

> ". . . they're goin' to pass laws that make the ones *extant* look like rules for a Sunday School picnic. They goin' to lock up the niggers in a black cellar and throw away the key. . . . I reckon you didn't figure on that either?"
>
> "No," I said, looking into his eyes, "if that be true. No."

And again:

> "Because, Reverend, basically speaking and in the pro-foundest sense of the word, you was a flat-assed *failure* —a total fiasco from beginning to end insofar as any real accomplishment is concerned. Right?"

As always, Nat Turner agrees, cowering in the posture of a guilt-ridden dog: "I felt myself shivering as I gazed down-ward between my legs. . . ."

In this, Styron's novel expresses faithfully white Amer-icans' reaction to black militancy, preaching to the dispossessed about the moral superiority and practical wisdom of nonviolence, as they arm the police with nerve-gas grenades, tanks and helicopter gunships. Their motto is *our violence pays, yours doesn't*.

Nothing could inspire such duplicity but unacknowledged dread. From this profoundest novel on slavery which also sheds a dazzling light on America's present, one element is conspicuously missing: white fear.

Herbert Aptheker's *American Negro Slave Revolts* records much interesting evidence of the fear which was in fact bound to possess the slave owners and their families. State governors, military commanders and slave masters corresponded incessantly to warn one another of actual or rumored conspiracies and acts of violence; other letters and diaries described plantation owners barricaded for the night with guns at the ready, as their wives tried to sleep with loaded pistols under the pillow, vigilantes scouring the countryside, and Southern towns looking like armed camps, with sentries, patrols in the streets and curfew at sundown. The whites may have talked about Negro docility, but they sure as hell weren't betting their lives on it. Yet Styron's rebel slave only once observes any sign of fright in his masters, in response to a half-crazed Negro's shouting. Immediately after the rebellion there is some panic among the foolhardy, which Gray describes as "safely laid to rest," but in Nat Turner's recollections there is nothing to suggest that fear was at all times endemic in slave-owning society.

Again, what appals here is not Styron's denial of history (there is nothing wrong with historical falsehoods which allow a work to be truthful within its fictional framework, as in, let's say, *Richard III*) but his denial of human nature—the total failure of sensibility that allows him to conceive human relationships (at whatever place or time) in which some men can *own* other men in the utmost comfort and safety, troubled, if at all, only by their consciences and the weather.

Commentary

"A SUPERB NOVEL . . . AN IMMENSE UNDERSTANDING OF THE HUMAN SPIRIT" John Thompson
Vogue

"THE FINEST AMERICAN NOVEL PUBLISHED IN MANY YEARS" Arthur Schlesinger, Jr.

The New York Review of Books

"WILLIAM FAULKNER'S NEGROES ARE STILL TO SOME EXTENT THE WHITE MAN'S NEGROES, STYRON'S ARE STARKLY THEMSELVES. . . . THIS REPRESENTS A RADICAL DEPARTURE FROM PAST WRITING ABOUT NEGROES, EVEN A BREAKTHROUGH. . . . STYRON THOROUGHLY EXPLORED THE NEGRO MILITANT'S HATRED OF WHITES. . . . IT IS THE FIRST TIME A WHITE WRITER HAS FACED UP TO THIS "PURE" AND OBDURATE HATRED, WHICH CAN ON NO ACCOUNT BE PERCEIVED BY THE SLAVEOWNERS IF THEY ARE TO PRESERVE THEIR SELF-RIGHTEOUSNESS OR EVEN ORDINARY EQUANIMITY. . . . IT SUGGESTS ANALOGUES WITH THE PRESENT THAT ARE VIVID AND URGENT" Philip Rahv

Nat Turner, the obdurate hater of whites, describes as *saintly* his second owner, who sells many of his slaves to the chain gangs, to die of work and fever on the cotton plantations of the Deep South (the saintly man *needs the money*), and who breaks his solemn promise to free Nat, passing him along instead to a loathsome Baptist minister. The Reverend Eppes, who not only tries to rape Nat but also works him twenty hours a day and rents him out to members of the congregation, is the master whom the slave rebel describes as *tolerable*, if barely. Exploring the black militant's racism, Styron finds that it contains the sympathetic insights of a Southern white novelist.

One wonders how critics would react to a German novel, *The Confessions of a Jew in Auschwitz*, in which the hero, shortly before he is taken to the gas chamber, remembers his masters with that kind of solicitude, talking about saintly Nazis possessed of "awesome goodness" and drawing fine distinctions between "truly respectable" and not-so-respectable SS officers. So far as I know, no German novelist has yet sunk as low as the American liberal literati, but one can see the appeal of the idea. It's so comforting to think that even those who hate us *understand* us, even our victims sympathize with the compelling necessities which oblige us to persecute them.

But Styron carries the notion of understanding and compassionate hatred beyond all known limits. This is how the fictional Nat Turner recalls his feelings just before he tries (but miraculously fails) to strike his owner with an ax:

> . . . I turned back to Travis now, and in doing so I realized with wonder that this was the first moment in all the years I had been near him that I had ever looked directly into his eyes. I had heard his voice, known his presence *like that of close kin;* . . . Now I saw that beneath the perplexity, the film of sleep, his eyes were brown and rather melancholy, acquainted with hard toil, remote perhaps, somewhat inflexible but *not at all unkind,* and *I felt that I knew him at last . . . Whatever else he was, he was a man.* [My italics.]

Turner's abhorrence of all whites gives way to irresolution (I beg your pardon, to his essential goodness) once he perceives that his owner is a man. And what a man! When three slaves show up in his bedroom in the middle of the night with broadax and hatchets, he is merely perplexed; and while his wife moans with terror, he looks at them with eyes *not at all unkind*. That's better than saintly, I should say. Only a raving homicidal maniac like Will could possibly harm such a slave master.

It is interesting, by the way, to read the real Nat Turner's own account of how Will came to join the rebellion:

> I saluted them on coming up, and asked Will how came he there, he answered, his life was worth no more than others, and his liberty as dear to him. I asked him if he meant to obtain it? He said he would, or loose his life. This was enough to put him in full confidence.

This is what novelist Styron makes of it:

> It was just after I had risen from my knees that I heard a rustling in the underbrush behind me and turned to see the demented, murderous, hate-ravaged, mashed-in face of Will. . . . "You git on out of here," I said. "We don' need no more men." . . . "Don' *shit* me, preacher man!" he said. . . . "I gwine git me some meat now—*white* meat. I gwine git me some dat white cunt too."

As Styron sees it, when black militancy is mad enough for murder, it is inspired not so much by rage and despair as by a panting lust for white cunt. Will not only butchers the first white man for his leader, he straightaway jumps on the first white woman.

> Will had just begun, his lust was so voracious as to be past all fathoming. . . . in a single leap he was across the bed and astride the screaming, squirming fat woman, friendly soul . . . this scarred, tortured little black man

was consummating at last ten thousand old swollen moments of frantic and unappeasable desire. Between Miss Sarah's thrashing, naked thighs he lay in stiff elongate quest like a lover; his downward-seeking head masked her face and mostly hid it—all but for the tangled tresses of her hair and the pupil of one eye, wildly quivering, which cast me a glint of lunatic blankness even as the hatchet went up again, and down, and chopped off her scream. Then unimaginable blood spewed forth and I heard the inhabiting spirit leave her body; it flew past my ear like a moth. . . . *"Ah my God!"* I thought, half aloud. *"Hast Thou truly called me to this?"*

A volume would be needed to describe what is wrong with this sadomasochistic rape fantasy, in which the blood is unimaginable but the departing soul is heard flying past Turner's ear to relieve the reader's shock of incredulity with a spiritual touch. But what is more interesting is that here Styron improves even on the Southern historians who sought but *failed to find* any indication of rape or attempted rape in the course of the Turner rebellion. (One of them, R. R. Howison, quoted by Aptheker, speculated desperately: "Remembering the brutal passion of the negro we can only account for this fact by supposing the actors to have been appalled by the very success of their hideous enterprise.")

The synthesis of the meek, gentle Negro of brutal passions is a prime specimen of kaleidoscopic delusion, in which the inspirations of suppressed fear mingle with the self-justifications of the slave masters for their sexual use of their female properties. As the slaves weren't in a position to talk back to a white woman, let alone touch her, the rapist image of the Negro can only be traced to the raping of black women by white men—a projection of guilt into the soul of the victim, prompted by the fear of retribution in kind. Styron gives us the modern, liberal version of the ancient bogeyman, as the poor "scarred, tortured little black man."

Needless to say, the novelist sees Turner's own rebellion as significantly dominated by his longing for a white virgin —Turner is made to daydream about raping her "with abrupt, brutal, and rampaging fury" and shooting into her "warm outrageous spurts of defilement" and, later, "warm milky spurts of desecration."

He despises his own sperm, which could only defile and desecrate a white girl; Styron protects the honor of Southern womanhood even within the slave leader's skull. Nat Turner is given to see that the white master he wants to kill is a man just like himself, but the white girl must always appear to him as a member of a different species. So she is the only person he finds himself capable of killing, and the novel crowns the Southampton Insurrection of 1831 with a kind of ritual sex murder.

> *Ah, how I want her,* I thought, and unsheathed my sword.

He stabs her twice and before he beats her head to a pulp with a fence rail, she looks at him "with a grave and drowsy tenderness." But this is not yet the end of the affair. Moments before his execution, Turner is still dreaming about making love with her—now, at last, on a footing of equality:

> . . . with tender stroking motions I pour out my love within her; pulsing flood; she arches against me, cries out, and the twain—black and white—are one.

(*134*)

This vision of racial harmony is followed by regret and remorse for the murder, because the prattling Southern maiden somehow (in a scene Styron shrewdly omits from the novel) communicated to the slave preacher a true knowledge of God (*"I would have spared her that showed me Him whose presence I had not fathomed or maybe never even known"*). What a reassuring dream of a Negro militant, so full of sex and piety even as he is being executed—and shortly before his skin is turned into a purse, if not a lampshade. Such people will forgive us our sewage plants.

Wall Street Journal
"WILLIAM STYRON HAS WRITTEN THE TRUE AMERICAN TRAGEDY. . . . THERE CAN BE NO DOUBT, NOW, THAT HE IS THE FOREMOST WRITER OF HIS GENERATION IN AMERICAN FICTION." Edmund Fuller

The New Statesman
"CERTAINLY HE'S WRITTEN A MAJOR NOVEL. . . . A GAP IN AMERICA'S PICTURE OF ITS OWN EVOLUTION HAS BEEN FILLED." Ronald Bryden

Organized religion has been overtaken by culture as the most potent force spreading madness in society. And the complaint that television serials, films, magazines or books don't measure up to conventional standards of artistic or social decorum only obscures the ravages they inflict on the brain. In fact, the churches, blamed for so many public crimes and private miseries, never had the stranglehold on people's time, attention, imagination and credulity that organized culture has today.

The absurdities of entertainment and false art are often defended on the grounds that hardly anybody takes them seriously, but this supposition is belied by the absurd attitudes and expectations so manifest in the state of the world. In the age of leisure, people amuse themselves into the depths of psychosis. So aesthetics becomes a number one mental health problem, and not only or even mainly in relation to the products manufactured for mass consumption. The mass fare is but the wide-screen projection of highbrow culture, which is all the more insidious for being less suspect.

Best sellers are Gallup polls on our psychological attitudes and—in the sense of what it both reveals and reinforces—Styron's novel can be justly considered a "true American tragedy." More specifically, it illustrates the tragedy of "serious" literature which, just like the cheapest kind, is used mainly to assuage our fears and anxieties and minister to our delusions. A small if poisonous event in itself, the book exposes the profound vacuity of the literary establishment which so enthusiastically championed it and explodes the myth of an elite and an elitist culture which we like to think are less subject to insensibility, unreason and ignorance than the rest of us. The novel's preposterousness casts less shame on William Styron (who had less chance to look at it with detachment) than on the learned critics and journals whose integrity and perceptive judgments we are all inclined to regard as indispensable— for information, if nothing else. Of course, the awesome badness of Styron's novel is no longer literary news; friends write from America that there had been a great many second thoughts by the time it received the Pulitzer Prize. The cultural establishment backs away from its misjudgments with unseemly haste, covering up the evidence of its incompetence and corruption, keeping its reputation intact to spread the good news of next year's rubbish. Politicians can never quite recover from the kind of indecent blunders literary experts take in their stride. As the editor of one of the authoritative journals that proclaimed the book a masterpiece wrote to me, "certainly it has been overpraised." *They* know—there's no need to refer to it again.

But the British quality journals (with *The Observer, The Times Literary Supplement*, and *The Times* as notable exceptions) reacted with only slightly less enthusiasm; and judging by the rave reviews for other awful books, the difference can be attributed less to British common sense than to the fact that these islands are not immediately threatened by a Negro revolution. Nor would it be difficult to find almost equally bad novels which have won the Prix Goncourt or the Nobel Prize by pandering to some national or international neurosis. It seems that wisdom and even taste in the arts are the prizes of courage—the courage to think unpalatable thoughts and refuse to daydream ourselves out of our predicaments; and since such courage is as rare among the educated caste as in any other social group, both highbrow and lowbrow literature consist mainly of what Stendhal called "universal cant."

Of course simple cant is not enough, and Styron's novel, 1968's annual American masterpiece, had to fulfill both the material and formal requirements of serious rubbish. The first requirement is a serious subject. Nothing is more self-evident in art than the fact that quality depends on the treatment and not on the theme; anyone can see that Cézanne's *Still Life with Basket of Apples* is a better painting than Holman Hunt's *The Light of the World*. Yet even in painting, subject has been playing havoc with quality most of the time. In the Soviet Union a portrait of a Worker is still thought to be more worthy than a nonrepresentational canvas, while in Western countries for decades nothing could be considered a significant work of art if it included recognizable human figures, which happened to be in disrepute. The same sort of approach has poisoned literary education: schoolchildren are asked what is the theme of a novel, not whether what it *reveals* about its theme is true or interesting, and universities increasingly present literature as a subsection of sociology, political science, moral philosophy or history. So readers and critics assume that any book with a big, important subject is ipso facto a big, important work, and a novel about a Negro slave uprising, which fills a gap in American history, just has to be a monumental achievement. The fact is, of course, that important subjects, for the very reason that we're so anxious about them, call forth the greatest amount of willful or unwitting nonsense. And so we have this absurd situation: it is difficult to imagine Styron writing quite such an appalling book on any subject *other* than a Negro slave rebellion, yet his novel couldn't possibly have received half as much acclaim if it had been on some "slighter" theme. The decisive question is, "What is the book *about?*" What it actually *says* on the subject hardly seems to matter.

Another requirement, connected with the first, is to take the name of the Almighty in vain. There are few pages in this 428-page volume that are not adorned with a quotation from the Bible or at least a mention of God; and although just as much frivolous and superficial nonsense has been written about the longings of the spirit as about anything else, I've read few dismissive reviews of any novel that invoked the protection of the Lord. Styron prefaces his narrative in which all the main characters murder and/or are murdered (and live only to suffer until they are cut off) with the biblical text: "And God shall wipe away all tears from their eyes; and there shall be no more death, neither sorrow, nor crying, neither shall there be any more pain: for the former things are passed away." Just the proper angle from which to view a spectacle of sorrow, pain, and death without getting too upset. On the final page, after Turner's hanging ("Surely I come quickly. Amen. Even so, come, Lord Jesus. Oh how bright and fair the morning star . . .") there is a resolute facing of facts (the information that Turner's corpse was skinned, grease made from his flesh and a purse from his hide), followed immediately by another and final consolation from the Bible: ". . . He that overcometh shall inherit all things . . ."

As most people are aware of their fear of truth, the serious novelist must provide them with the illusion that they're brave enough to overcome it, without actually forcing them to do so. So Styron presents us with a tale of horror, but is unfailingly solicitous toward his sensitive readers (or rather toward himself—the novel is evidently inspired by an authentic failure of nerve). If the sedative idea of painless immortality isn't enough, there is the extra protection of the words: whatever happens, happens behind a thick curtain of richly embroidered prose. For any kind of style to work, it must be consistent, and Styron is shooting for the smallest events with his biggest descriptions. Ordinary Christians may just not feel in the mood for prayer, but this is how Styron's lay preacher from the backwoods of Virginia goes about not praying:

Prayer again hovered at the margin of my consciousness, prowling there restlessly like some great gray cat yearning for entry into my mind. Yet once again prayer remained outside and apart from me, banned, excluded, unattainable, shut out as decisively as if walls as high as the sun had been interposed between myself and God. So instead of prayer I began to whisper aloud . . .

Even the adjectives fear the light of day: not daring to appear on their own, they come in droves with their companions from the thesaurus. Styron unites all the synonyms.

There is, of course, a great deal of compassion in the book (serious rubbish must testify to the author's deep humanity), and the very words are wet with Styron's tears as he flies away on wings of sorrow from the realities he has no heart to imagine or understand. In fact, he cares so little for Turner's suffering that he squanders not just his own but *Turner's* pity on the hanging judge and the court's lawyer, the two men directly responsible for his execution. In the death cell, recalling his only previous encounter with Judge Jeremiah Cobb, he remembers with deep appreciation the anguished look on Cobb's face as he pondered the slaves' sufferings and his anguished cry ("Great God! Sometimes I think . . . sometimes . . . *it is like living in a dream!*") as he stood by and watched a slave being driven up a tree. Nat decided then, ". . . this man Cobb will be among those few spared the sword"; and his devotion does not flag just because Cobb condemns him to death. This is the moment right after the passing of the sentence:

> We gazed at each other from vast distances, yet close, awesomely close, as if sharing for the briefest instant some rare secret—unknown to other men—of all time,

all mortality and sin and grief. In the stillness the stove
howled and raged . . .

Before the reader can unravel the puzzle of this intense
mutual sympathy between the hanging judge and his prisoner, a new mystery is hinted at, a rare secret between the
two, a secret unknown to other men, including, I'm sure,
Styron himself. (In point of fact, the secrets of those who
are condemned to death and those who condemn them are
poles apart. But of course it all makes sense as the execu-
tioner's daydream projected into the victim.)

As for the court's lawyer, Nat doesn't cotton to him
much during the interrogation, but he changes his mind at
the end when Gray brings him a Bible. The advocate of
slavery turns out to be a decent fellow, deep down.

> "I brung you what you asked for, Reverend," he says in
> a soft voice. So composed does he seem, so tranquil, so
> gentle are his tones, that I almost take him for another
> man. "I done it against the will of the court. It's my
> doing, my risk. . . ."

Having witnessed the apparition of executioners with
hearts of gold, Nat Turner, in his last moments, not only
pities Judge Cobb for his personal misfortunes (the Judge
is bereaved of his wife and daughters and is "about to cash
in hisself") but is even made to pity Gray, a contented man
in perfect health, for simply being *alive:* "I feel a wrench of
pity for Gray and for his mortal years to come."

That's how it is throughout the book—people torture
and suffer, kill and die, with the utmost mutual compassion.
It's love that makes the world go round.

Styron reminds me of the Humanist in Sartre's *Nausea,*
who is in love with the idea of loving people but never pays

any attention to them. In Thomas Mann's *Doctor Faustus*, Adrian asks his friend: "Do you think love is the greatest emotion?" "Why, do you know a greater one?" "Yes," answers Adrian, "interest."

Interest is the last thing we're willing to grant to one another, for the more we know about others the more we're forced to recognize that they're not extensions of ourselves. We love people with all our hearts so long as we can conceive them as shadows in the universe which centers around us, shadows dominated by our sensations and feelings, not their own. This is how the baby loves: his mother isn't yet a separate entity, so when he's sucking her breast he's filling her too; hence the bitter crying, the rage of incomprehension when she doesn't feel his hunger—a part of his own being is letting him down. Eventually we learn to appreciate to some degree the separate identity of other people (to what degree can be measured by our irritation when someone laughs while we're depressed). But the bully hasn't grown at all; he still loves like an infant, refusing to grant others their independent existence.

Styron's phony literary compassion is the bully's love, for it falls short of the minimal recognition of other human beings, the recognition that, for each man, the most real thing is what happens to *him*. By presenting a fantasy world in which people's attitudes are uninfluenced by their own immediate sensations of pain and terror, the book encourages our worst yet inescapable inclination to assume that other people are *not quite real*. It becomes an incitement to the madness it so chillingly exemplifies, luring the reader into the psychotic dreamland where all humanity is rooted in his own ego.

This is the home state of America's violence. The more

we obliterate the identity of others by projecting our feelings into them, the less we can tolerate their insistence on asserting themselves and breaking the spell. And this, ultimately, is what drives the assassin to aim at public figures: they are so flagrantly different, they are so evidently not part of him, he can no longer project himself into them except through the barrel of a rifle.

The delusions which urge us to violence contain also our absolution. The complete separation of people's feelings and thoughts from what they're actually doing or what is happening to them, which is so central to all the other falsehoods in the book, is also the most sought-after lie in all literature. The leader of a murderous rebellion who is at the same time a most gentle and sensitive fellow, and the slave masters who thus appear through his eyes in the full regalia of their self-justifications, alike provide fictitious proof that one's actions have nothing to do with one's true nature, affirming the reader's innocence whatever his crimes may be.

Notions like these must be clothed in obscurity. Styron's novel is filled with portentous words of no particular meaning, like "vast," "awesome" and "rare"; and the more imprecise the word, the more frequent its use. On two successive pages I counted eight versions of "mystery" (including a profound mystery, a great mystery, a tranquil and abiding mystery and "something mysterious, ineffable and without name"). And there are, of course, the "visions," the "dreams" and the "secrets" only hinted at. All these, along with the synonyms, serve to create a general impression of sublimity and profundity, to satisfy those who like to read *deep books* if they can do so without the trouble of thinking. More important, however, is the aid and comfort such words give to the self-deceptions of both author and reader.

This novel may be seen as a warning to us all: whenever our wishful thinking is contradicted by the evidence of our senses, we are tempted to hide the contradictions under the blanket of inscrutability.

The more we lie to ourselves, the more we believe in mysteries.

One of the Very Few

TRUE GREATNESS is like infinity, we cannot measure it. As a rule, attempts to assess works of art impair even our ability to experience them. Treating creative achievements as if they were sociological or historical surveys or exercises in pious intentions, much of literary scholarship is employed in destroying the vital distinction between the ordinary and the extraordinary—in the kind of barbaric incomprehension that would describe a woman's glance by saying that she had twenty-twenty vision. Yet this pedestrian *seriousness*, which Stendhal was the first to recognize as the malignancy of modern culture, dominates teaching to this day, with the result that only readers with indestructible sensibilities can possibly survive becoming educated about literature. Literary education is the chief instrument for alienating the young from good writing, and particularly from the classics. The pedantic lectures about this or that novelist's brilliant portrayal of a bygone age, in which hardly anyone is interested, propagate the fallacy that the great writers of the past wrote about things dead and gone.

But calumny is truth misapplied. What gives deadly credibility to the socio-historic-moralistic mistreatment of literary works of art is the abundance of dated novelists who were little more than chroniclers of their society and righteous spokesmen of its delusions. Such writers suffered, if not from lack of talent, then from an overdose of their solidified culture and its conventions. Orwell said of Dickens's characters that they were prototypes of their trade or class rather than individuals, representing social functions rather than particular human beings. The same could be said of most fiction written in England or elsewhere in periods of real or apparent social stability when people's roles and relationships were preordained and permanent, and even their feelings, thoughts and motives were expected to conform to defined patterns. In a world where everyone knows his place, few have a chance to know themselves, let alone others; when people are typecast for life, the performance becomes indistinguishable from the actors. Again, it is Orwell who points out that Dickens, though a deeply compassionate man and a radical by the standards of his age, presented his "good" lower-class characters as blissfully content with their station: the poor may bewail starvation but not poverty, the servant may resent his treatment but not his servitude. Indeed, many Victorian novelists' ill-famed portrayal of sex is matched only by their equally false and spiteful denigration of social ambition: the antithesis of the contented servants and saintly wives is that heinously maligned character, Becky Sharp.

At such times human desires which transcend the status

quo—the most lively, best inspirations of our nature—are considered evil, because they reach beyond the realm of conceivable possibility. As Thackeray, for all his unwilling admiration of Becky's charm and spunk, sees her determination to rise in the world as proof of her essential wickedness, so Flaubert conceives Madame Bovary, who longs to escape from a loveless and dreary marriage, as a vulgar woman whose emotional ambition can only be stupid and destructive. The point is not that these writers weren't radical: a romantic revolutionary like Victor Hugo or a radical social critic like Ibsen suffers from the same superficiality when he defines his characters in opposition to their social roles. When people tend to appear only in a certain standard way (within not only a rigid social system but also within a rigid ideology like late-nineteenth-century determinism in western Europe), it is difficult to get to know them. Social stagnation poisons perception down to the minutest false details, for it makes people appear only as their moral, ideological, or social functions. And this is so because we observe only what we expect to see; the unexpected is unnoticed, denied, or condemned. When too many things are taken for granted, it is next to impossible to perceive the truth.

Thus even many of the "classics" lose their appeal as soon as the world is transformed, as soon as we alter our expectations of how people should feel and behave. We are forever disinclined to differentiate between what *is* and what we think ought or ought not to be (desire and fear being our chief advisers), but we prefer our falsehoods to be contemporary.

This is said not to offend the dead but to separate them from the living—and to suggest the advantage enjoyed by those independent spirits who have sought to understand reality at times of political upheaval and drastic social change, when they could experience the relativity of appearances and governing ideologies. It is when no one's position is safe and no idea can be taken for granted that truths about our existence are allowed to surface. Danger is the muse of fiction. It is under her spell that we find those writers who (with luck to their genius) penetrated beyond the social paraphernalia, beyond the slanted visions of their age, and re-created our destinies as if seen through the eyes of God. Stendhal was one of these very few: he wrote in the eternal present tense.

No other great prose writer, in fact, had quite his opportunities to catch people between their acts, to perceive the actors behind their text and performance. Marie-Henri Beyle, whom we know as Stendhal, was born in 1783, in Grenoble. His father was a pious, prosperous and fanatically royalist lawyer, and the family home, dominated by the spirit of feudal France, was appropriately situated in the rue des Vieux-Jésuites. Young Beyle was five years old when Louis XVI's France declared itself bankrupt, six when the Revolution erupted—his tenth birthday fell not on 23 January 1793 but (retroactively) on 3 pluviôse, I, the year when the King was executed and Christianity officially abolished. Of all these events the changing calendar may seem the least cataclysmic, yet what is so matter of course, so natural, as our way of marking dates? Consider suddenly being told that this was Frostymonth of year II, and not the end of the month but the beginning—from then on you would be wary of taking anything for granted. It was thus that young Beyle became used to momentous surprises, which abound in his great novels. At sixteen he left Grenoble to study in Paris, and entered the capital for the first time on 19 brumaire—the day after General Bonaparte, the defender of the Revolution, overthrew the Directory of the Revolution.

Thanks to the patronage of Pierre Daru, his distant cousin and one of Napoleon's chief aides, Beyle spent the greater part of the next fourteen years in Napoleon's orbit, first as a junior officer and later as an administrator, through twelve campaigns, from the triumphal entries into Milan, Berlin, and Vienna to the burning of Moscow and the retreat of 1812. He witnessed the rise and fall of the great Bonapartist heroes and potentates and saw many of them rise again as craven courtiers to the vengefully renascent Bourbons (*"ces Bourbons imbéciles à faire vomir"*) and survive unscathed when Charles X himself was overthrown in 1830. Beyle watched the July Revolution from the arcades of the Théâtre Français, having seen his contemporaries play all the parts available in the human comedy.

Under the new constitutional monarch, Citizen King Louis-Philippe (no less despised as *"le plus fripon des Kings"*) he was appointed to the consulate of Civitavecchia: Beyle, who had no illusions left about the world, ended his life, fittingly, as a diplomat. On 22 March 1842 he collapsed on the street in Paris, never to recover consciousness. During his fifty-nine years he had lived under ten regimes in France and six different constitutions, and had been known as a "cynic"; he took nothing on trust and passed on no lies.

The classic example of his lightning exposé of social reality is his portrayal of the battle of Waterloo at the beginning of *The Charterhouse of Parma*. "He has created only a few episodes of this rout," wrote Balzac in his review, "but so suggestive are his brushstrokes that the mind sees beyond the given details, taking in the whole battlefield." Later Tolstoy said that he learned from Stendhal how to describe battles, how to disregard the grandeur of armies for the experience of individuals. But not even *War and Peace* has a scene as poignant as the Waterloo in *Charterhouse*. Stendhal conveys it through a description of sixteen-year-old Fabrizio del Dongo's enthusiastically fumbling attempts to join Napoleon's last stand for an egalitarian Europe. At the end, Fabrizio isn't even certain whether he has been in that glorious battle, as he has seen only smoke, confusion, a friendly *vivandière* with her little cart, stragglers bargaining for horses and food, shooting, stealing, maiming—and the mysterious spectacle of people who have suddenly ceased to live.

Through the buildup and letdown of Fabrizio's expectations, Stendhal can make us see not only beyond the details of the battle but beyond the confines of the period, beyond the glittering slogans and delusions that unite men in self-destruction. The solitary corpses on the field of Waterloo are the foundation of the principality of Parma, a totalitarian state that belongs to all ages. But it is, to use Valéry's phrase, one of the "characteristic magnitudes" of Stendhal's whole *œuvre* to show the world in the light of this truth: each man is alone in history.

It was in Civitavecchia that he wrote an account of his childhood and youth as *The Life of Henry Brulard*. Quite apart from its merit as a report on the making of a genius, it is a most amusing masterpiece, deserving all the praise so mistakenly heaped upon Rousseau's ponderous *Confessions*. In English, only Bertrand Russell's joyous irony can give any idea of its lighthearted spirit, the offhand sincerity and easy clarity that the stupid mistake for shallowness. Readers of *Henry Brulard* could pursue further the parallels between these two enemies of humbug; here it is perhaps enough to mention that both grew up without friends of their own age, in the company of "strangers." Stendhal was seven when he lost his mother, whom he loved so passionately that her death seems to have destroyed every trace of filial sympathy for his father. As he recalls in the book, he overheard the priest saying that Mme Beyle's death was the Will of God, an opinion with which the bereaved husband piously concurred; and that took care of both God and Beyle *père*, as far as young Henri was concerned. From then on, his lifelong aversion to "little white lies" was hardened by constant exposure to the pretensions and hypocrisies of his father and Aunt Séraphie, who came to take his mother's place—relatives he could not identify with and had no wish to excuse.

When a family servant died, the aunt was worried about little Henri mourning him too excessively:

> Séraphie, seeing me crying for poor Lambert, had a row with me. I marched out to the kitchen, muttering as if to revenge myself on her: "Infamous, infamous!"

In a household of *ultras*, he became a staunch republican. Here is his account of a family scene that took place after Chérubin Beyle was arrested and released by the kindly representatives of the "Reign of Terror" in Grenoble:

> Two or three months after this incident, which my family never stopped complaining about, I let slip an

innocent remark which confirmed my wicked character. They were expressing, in their genteel way, the horror they felt at the mere mention of Amar's name.

"But," I said to my father, "Amar put you down on the list as notoriously *suspect* of not loving the Republic. It seems to me certain that you do not love it."

At this, the whole family turned crimson with indignation. They nearly locked me up in my bedroom; and during supper, which was announced shortly afterwards, no one addressed a single word to me. I pondered deeply over this. Nothing could be truer than what I had said, my father gloried in execrating *the new order of things* (a fashionable expression among the aristocrats at the time)—so what right did they have to be indignant?

Children's pitiless common sense is proverbial, but most of them grow weary of using it in the face of adult protest. They fear rejection, retribution, or simply being wrong; so they cease to observe and learn to believe. Even when they think "differently" they tend to do so in groups, preferring to put their faith in shared opinion rather than in what they perceive to be true. Henri Beyle, however, remained stubbornly loyal to his own senses.

He is eleven when he forges a letter in the name of the commander of the revolutionary youth army, ordering Citizen Beyle to send his son to join *les bataillons de l'Espérance*, and deposits the paper at the door to the landing of a staircase *inside* the house. When he is found out, he is sent to his grandfather's study to wait for the verdict: in this royalist family, he is "in the moral position of a young deserter about to be shot":

> There I amused myself by tossing into the air a ball of red clay I had just molded. . . . The fact that I had committed forgery worried me a little.

(*152*)

When he is called to face his judges and is sentenced to three days' exile from the family table, he recovers his spirits:

> "I'd rather dine alone," I told them, "than with tyrants who never stop scolding me."

Apart from his secret qualms about the forgery, the account of Stendhal's boyhood doesn't record a single occasion on which he showed any sign of doubting himself just because everybody in sight disagreed with him, while he is often shown simmering with rage because of his family's inability to grasp that "two and two make four" (one of his favorite and characteristic remarks). For two years, Henri also wages a relentless war against his detested tutor, the Jesuit abbé Raillane, who insists on teaching him Ptolemaic astronomy because "it explains everything and is also approved by the Church."

> When we went for walks along the Isère . . . he used to take me aside and explain to me how imprudent I was in my speech. "But, sir," I used to say to him, in effect, "it is true, it's the way I feel."
> "Never mind about that, my little friend, you must not say it, it will not do."

But it was the Jesuit's advice that would not do for Henri, and he remained imprudent all his life. Scholars to this day reproach him for his insufferable arrogance. True, it is the stuff impervious fanatics are made of, but it is also a vital attribute for people who know how to count. Without that wicked self-conceit, no artist could maintain the courage of his insights, the daring to create, to play God.

Already, at the age of seven, he has decided he will grow up "to write comedies like Molière and live with an actress." Fortified by his future glory, by the Revolution, by his reading (*Don Quichotte, Les Liaisons Dangereuses*), he "breathes revolt" and resolves to excel in his beloved mathematics because "it will get him out of Grenoble." Finally, at the turn of the century and the Lausanne Gate, he mounts a horse to start on his decisive journey to Italy with the First Consul's triumphant army. He has never had a riding lesson, but doesn't think that he can't ride just because he hasn't learned how, or at any rate it doesn't occur to him that he should confess his ignorance and ask for advice; so he leaps on a mean-tempered beast which goes berserk under him and gallops across a field of willows, heading for Lake Geneva. An officer's orderly pursues them around the field for a quarter of an hour and, after a perilous struggle in which he risks breaking his own neck, brings the horse to a halt. By way of thanks, the pale young man questions his rescuer with regal disdain: "What do you want?"

Yet what is pride but a keen sense of solitude? Henri cannot admit that he needed help, because he cannot conceive of anyone wishing to give him a helping hand. He even suspects the orderly of saving his life only to arrest him, and thinks of drawing his pistols. Clearly, life is going to be a fight between H.B. and the world. He is to be his own hero.

Still, how unlike Stendhal, the dreariness of most independent spirits! He fights with the world like an ardent lover with his mistress—none of her real or imagined slights can prevent him from loving her with all his heart. His joyful sensations are always keener than his bitterest thoughts.

> I wanted to cover my mother with kisses, wishing away
> all clothes. She loved me to distraction and used to hug

me all the time, and I returned her kisses with such fire that she was often obliged to draw away from me. I loathed my father when he came in and interrupted our kissing. I always wanted to kiss her on the breast. Kindly remember that I lost her in childbirth when I was scarcely seven years old.

This recollection in *Henry Brulard* is noted by many commentators as evidence of his "Oedipus complex"—an example of how Freudian asides miss the point. A "complex" is a manifestation of thwarted feelings, of conflict between impulse and some imperative norm of behavior, implying inhibition and guilt; nothing could be further from Stendhal. The love and charm of the woman closest to him prompt him to respond with his whole being; his senses, his emotions are too powerful to be managed by concepts, moral or otherwise; so he cannot react "selectively." The idea of "mother" can never be as real to him as the actuality of her physical being. His senses absorb the world so vividly that they etiolate all mental considerations. It is this that allows him to perceive and convey life in its *immediacy* (that is, in its reality) which for most of us is buried under concepts or clouded by emotions storming in the void of abstractions. But perhaps the easiest way to describe the unique is by its common opposite. People who can be overwhelmed by the mental image of dominoes while looking at maimed and dead Vietnamese manifest an incapacity to "receive" the world which is the exact antithesis of Stendhal's extraordinary ability to absorb the reality of each moment. After his mother's death he becomes bitter and moody, but he is quickly brought to life by all impressions—a vibrant breast, a beautiful landscape, or a song.

In the end, it is music, the language of the emotions, that acquaints him with his true nature. "I was truly born in La Scala," he records of his arrival in Milan. The opera, the then beautiful and spirited city, Renaissance art, women—all that Italy has to offer to a young aide-de-camp of a liberating army—awaken sensibilities unequaled in the history of the novel.

There is no clue about a gesture, a glance, an intonation, the mood of a scene that he will miss; and he will extend the limits of prose to realms that only music or the visual arts could reach. He will write volumes on both music and Italian art, and (although the best of these is his carelessly brilliant *Life of Rossini* and he compares his intentions to Correggio's) he could well be introduced to strangers as the Mozart and Botticelli of literature. Like Mozart, he re-creates life's passions in their full force yet without exaggeration and with the elegance of absolute precision (for great passions assert themselves with clarity and cannot mix with sentimentality). And his characters, like Botticelli's figures, are both real and *singular*. Stendhal, like Botticelli, can paint grace—which accounts for the magic of his women. He doesn't hesitate to repeat himself in describing the heroine of each of his three great novels (Mme de Rênal in *The Red and the Black*, Mme de Chasteller in *Lucien Leuwen*, the Duchessa Sanseverina in *The Charterhouse of Parma*) as "a woman whose beauty is the least of her charms." This description will make sense to anyone who has seen *The Birth of Venus*, even if he hasn't read the novels, and the memory of the painting can suggest to him the extra dimensions of Stendhal's art.

It is the fruit of a lifetime of passionate adventure. In Milan, the eighteen-year-old aide-de-camp falls in love promptly and hopelessly (the hopelessness is assumed, as he is too overwhelmed to make advances), but the sensation of proximity to Gina Pietragrua is exquisite bliss, as are the little affairs, the music of Cimarosa, plays and paintings, and animated conversation in the salons. Having experienced the rare sensation of "five or six months of divine, total happiness," he decides that it's the best thing in the world and dedicates the rest of his life to *la chasse au bonheur.*

It's an uphill struggle. The few exalted months end by his contracting venereal disease, a shock that would dampen any young man's spirits. Not Beyle's. "I'm horribly sick today," he writes in his *Journal.* "I shall go out tomorrow."

At the beginning of 1802, he returns to Grenoble on convalescent leave and promptly falls in love with Victorine, whom he follows to Paris in April, without leave from the army. As he recalls in one of the obituaries he wrote about himself, "The minister [Daru] was angry and B. resigned his commission." But Victorine is removed to Rennes with her family, and Beyle begins to court his fourteen-year-old Parisian cousin Adèle, until he succeeds with her mother instead. For three years he lives on a small allowance from his father and devotes his full time to reading, going to the theater and trying to write comedies. To get him to do some honest work, as he notes in the same obituary, "his father tried to starve him into submission. B., more determined than ever, set about studying how to become a great man." The plays don't come off but he achieves his second childhood ambition: the actress Mélanie Guilbert, who rejects him in Paris, becomes his mistress when he follows her to Marseilles and even takes a job with an exporter of foodstuffs to prove his devotion. In less than a year he is back in Paris, making his peace with Daru, and is dispatched on the emperor's service to Brunswick, where he pays court to Wilhelmina (a virtuous girl engaged to someone else) and hears for the first time *Così fan Tutte* and *Figaro*.

On an extended "assignment" in Paris, he gorges himself on the theater, books, conversation in the salons, dancing lessons, Spanish lessons, but after four months is ordered back to the war commissary in Strasbourg and follows the army to Vienna in the spring of 1809. Eventually he persuades Daru to attach him to Napoleon's court in the capital, as inspector of the royal households and furnishings, and enjoys a "brilliant year" in Paris in 1811, keeping an actress, Angeline Bereyter, and making a declaration of love to Daru's wife. Receiving a firm but friendly refusal, he travels to Milan to see his first hopeless love, Gina Pietragrua. This time he is lucky, leaves the next morning for Bologna, Florence, Rome, and Naples, and is inspired to write a history of Italian paintings. This happy interlude is followed by the Russian campaign, in which Beyle, always a bored but competent administrator, distinguishes himself as organizer of food supplies on the retreat from Moscow. "The farther he ran away from danger, the more it terrified him," he writes in another of his premature obituaries. "He reached Paris in a state of anguish, as much physical as mental. A month of good food, or rather of sufficient food, restored him." On Daru's insistence, he takes part in the campaign of 1813 in Poland, as intendant to "a most hidebound general," but falls ill with some pernicious fever and in a week is reduced to such a feeble state that he has to be sent home to France—only to steal his way back to Italy, to recover his health on Lake Como. He returns to the service, but when his career collapses with the Empire in 1814, he sells his apartment and furniture, carriage and horses, and catches the first stagecoach to Milan, to spend the next seven years in Italy, "the land of sensibilities."

The tempestuous affair with Pietragrua coming to an end, he meets in Milan's radical *carbonari* circles his most hopeless love of all, the haughty Mathilde Viscontini-Dembowski, who holds him at arm's length for three years. However, the Austrian police don't know what to make of this Frenchman who is so fond of the company of passionate and subversive Italians, and in 1821 they deliver him from Mathilde's tormenting presence by hounding him out of Milan. On his way back to Paris, he is wavering between the desire to kill himself and the fear that his friends will laugh at him:

> "What if the worst happens?" I cried out, "what if those dried-up friends of mine guess at my passion—and for a woman I haven't slept with!" . . . I entered Paris, which I found worse than ugly, an insult to my grief, with one single idea: *not to be found out.*
>
> *Memoirs of an Egotist*

He is thirty-eight years old at the time. Some of his contemporaries and future critics describe him as "a perpetual adolescent," "a child who never grew up"; like a child, he is the fool of all his impulses, too rash, too excitable, too much in the grip of his impressions to cope successfully with the world. Whatever he gets out of life, he has to go a long way for it and pay dearly. He's but a poor, sick, unlucky devil who makes a meager living from his books on music, painting, and travel and by writing reviews for

English journals. What could be a more painful sign of an all-around failure than the fact that, pushing forty, he can't wear a new coat without his friends suspecting that it was bought for him by a woman?

The bare facts of his life would indicate rather the making of a French Dostoevski, a man who has become an expert on suffering, on the crazy, stupefying whirlwind of emotions. To some it may seem pathetic that this man considers himself—both in his life and work—a success at *la chasse au bonheur*. Yet nothing sums him up with greater exactitude than his own credo:

> "Genius is the torch that lights the way to the art of happiness."

This great art, in fact, must rest on a keen awareness of life's miseries. For what relevance, what truth could there be in a happy-go-lucky ignorance of the sufferings which are our common destiny? Stendhal's genius is rooted in his refusal to paint mirages, in his rejection of the pretty daydreams that only increase our disappointments. As a seventeen-year-old soldier, on his way to Milan and the dedication to *bonheur*, he went through his first battle, in which he discovered that the true source of happiness was simply *being alive*; so he can embrace and in a way wring satisfaction out of everything that happens to him: the joy of surviving is his keenest pleasure. "To live is to feel, to have *powerful emotions*," he writes, which is not at all the self-evident insight it may seem. He submits to all sensations if they are intense enough: even deeply felt defeat is victory. What matters is to experience to the full the miracle of existing. (In this, too, he is akin to Mozart: his divine lightheartedness suggests all of man's sufferings.) It is a clue both to his character and his work that he correctly advises readers not to bother with him if they have never spent at least six months in the agonies of love.

The demonstration that our happiness depends on our actual feelings and not, as it is commonly supposed, on our situation, is another of Stendhal's characteristic magnitudes. In *The Charterhouse of Parma*, Fabrizio, the veteran of Waterloo, who is trying to make his fortune in Parma under orders from his adoring Aunt Gina and her lover the Prime Minister, and who eventually becomes an archbishop, is happiest where everyone expects him to be the most miserable—in prison. He falls in love with the prison governor's daughter and, to his great surprise, the mere glimpse of her through a hole in the wall turns out to be more fun than he has ever experienced in the world outside. For weeks Fabrizio foils all attempts at rescue, and even after his reluctant escape he longs to return to his cell in the Farnese Tower.

"Stock response," which is usually discussed in terms of aesthetics, is in truth one of the great problems of our lives: we continually *expect* ourselves to react in a certain way. We not only presume to foresee future events, we even presume to know our future feelings about them, and this is the source of much of our unhappiness. No writer can help to cure us of this self-inflicted misery so much as Stendhal; the novelist whom Freud called "a genius of psychology" shows the continuous tension in our consciousness between our expected and real reactions. One way to describe his first great novel, *The Red and the Black,* is to say that it is an ironic tale about a young man who is so determined to put himself in "happy situations," so certain he knows what will give him happiness, that he fails to notice when he actually *is* happy.

That we count on our stock responses is most evident in

our attitude to money. As for Stendhal, he was not only poor but "childishly" capricious and irresolute in his material ambitions. Despite his high standing in the Napoleonic era, his many contacts among the Old Guard and his willingness to use them, he could never persist in his attempts to get rich. Invited to *ask* for the post of director of provisioning in Paris under the Bourbons, he declared that he was in an admirable position to accept it. The man who did ask for the post retired after four years, "tired of making money." Stendhal spent this time in the country where "sunshine costs nothing," enriching his senses with music, art, the maddening Gina and the unattainable Mathilde.

The violent changes in the social order in France carried wave after wave of newcomers to power and riches, bringing "everything" to people who had thought that all they were missing in life was position and possessions. Their disappointment produced the first epidemic of the malaise that afflicts the suddenly affluent classes of today, the source of which is simply that we cannot make love with unresponsive objects, no matter how hopefully we labor to obtain them, no matter how we overlay them with sexual symbolism. We have a *static* relationship with whatever we possess; it is a spell of death. Stendhal had a profound understanding of this existential flaw in the prizes of the rat race. In the minor character of M. de Rênal, *The Red and the Black* portrays the frustrations of success in the minutest detail. Mayor of Verrières, rich manufacturer, rewarded and decorated as a loyal *ultra*, owner of the town's handsomest new house and most spacious gardens, an heiress wife and three sons, M. de Rênal is striving and continually failing to wring satisfaction out of his deals, honors, and acquisitions—like an unhappy fish in a silver bowl trying to find some way in which the preciousness of the container could make a difference to his swimming in the stagnant water of confined space.

Stendhal prefers to travel. During his jobless years in Paris, he contrives two more trips to England, three to Italy and a leisurely tour of the Midi as far south as Barcelona, mystifying his rich friends. Here is his description of one of them, the Baron Adolphe de Mareste:

> Lussinge, then aged thirty-six or thirty-seven, had the head of a man of fifty-five. He was moved profoundly only by events which touched him personally; then he went mad, as at the moment of his marriage. . . . He had a mother who was a miser but also quite demented and capable of giving everything she owned to the priests. He decided to get married; this would be an occasion for his mother to make pledges which would prevent her from giving her property to her confessor. . . . Finally he married a perfect dolt, big and quite handsome, if she had only had a nose. . . . With her dowry, his salary as an official of the Ministry of Police, his mother's endowments, Lussinge had an income of 22- or 23,000 pounds a year around 1828. From that moment, he was dominated by one single emotion: the *fear of losing*. Despising the Bourbons (not as I did, from political virtue, but despising them for their clumsiness), he got to the point where he couldn't hear about their blunders without flying into a rage. He had a sudden, blinding vision of danger to his property. . . . In our political discussions he used to say to me: "You—*you* have no fortune."

Stendhal immersed himself in company instead—how wholeheartedly can be gathered from the wit and verve he

(*163*)

brings to these portraits of his contemporaries in *Memoirs of an Egotist*. This is how he describes General Lafayette:

A great height, and on top of this tall body, an imperturbable visage, cold, impassive like an old family portrait, the head covered with a disheveled curly wig; this man, dressed in an ill-fitting gray coat, limping a little and leaning on a stick, entering the salon of Mme de Tracy (who called him, with an enchanting ring in her voice, *mon cher Monsieur*)—this was General de La Fayette in 1821.

That *cher Monsieur* of Mme de Tracy's (and said in that particular tone) caused, I think, some distress to M. de Tracy. It wasn't that M. de La Fayette had been intimate with the lady, nor was M. de Tracy, at his age, at all worried about that sort of thing; it was simply that the sincere, unforced, and unassumed admiration of Mme de Tracy for M. de La Fayette made him too evidently the most important person in the salon.

Novice though I was in 1821 (I had always lived in the illusions of enthusiasm and passion), I worked that out *all by myself*.

I sensed also, without being told, that M. de La Fayette was, quite simply, a Plutarch hero. He lived from day to day, without too much *esprit*, and like Epaminondas, performed whatever great action presented itself to him. And in the meantime, in spite of his age (he was born in 1757, like Charles X, with whom he took the Tennis Court Oath in 1789), he was singlemindedly devoted to putting his hand up the skirt of every pretty girl, without the slightest embarrassment and as often as possible.

While waiting around for great actions, which don't present themselves every day, and for the opportunity to fondle bottoms, which hardly occurs till after midnight, M. de La Fayette expounded, without too much elegance, the commonplaces of the National Guard. A good government—and the only good government—is one which guarantees the citizen safety on the highway, equality before the judge (and a fairly enlightened judge), the money he's entitled to, passable roads, fair protection abroad. So arranged, the matter isn't too complicated. . . .

As for me, accustomed to Napoleon and Lord Byron (and, I might add, Lord Brougham, Monti, Canova, Rossini), I immediately recognized greatness in M. de La Fayette and never changed my opinion. I saw him during the July Revolution with his shirt in tatters; he welcomed all the intriguers, all the fools, everyone who made a bombastic approach to him. He was not so cordial to me—he plucked me and gave my post to a vulgar secretary, M. Levasseur. It never entered my head to be angry with him or to venerate him less, any more than it would have occurred to me to blaspheme against the sun when it was covered by a cloud.

M. de La Fayette, at the tender age of seventy-five, has the same failing I have. He is now infatuated with a young Portuguese, eighteen years old, a member of M. de Tracy's salon and a friend of his daughters . . . He thinks of no one but her, he imagines that this young Portuguese (and every other young woman) will favor him, and the amusing thing is, he is often quite right.

Stendhal can afford to be generous to Lafayette. For six years, by his own account, his hopeless love for Mathilde Dembowski plunges him into despairing celibacy, but when he recovers in 1824, he takes as his mistress one of the most desirable women in France, the Comtesse Clémentine Curial. ("It was Clémentine who caused me the greatest misery when she left me . . . she was the wittiest of them all.") Several affairs later, while he is writing *The Red and the Black*, a young Sienese lady living in Paris, Giulia Rinieri, falls in love with him (he is forty-seven, poor, fat, gouty, and intermittently syphilitic) and he requests her hand in marriage. Her guardian-uncle, the Tuscan ambassador, suggests a brief postponement.

Though he is regarded as a dangerous liberal—Metternich personally vetoes his appointment to Trieste in 1830, and he is lucky to obtain even the consulate of Civitavecchia—he continually risks his job by abandoning it for months at a time, visiting Naples, Florence, Siena, the Abruzzi, Bologna, Ravenna, going on archaeological digs in the Roman countryside. Granted sick leave for three months, he stays away for three years, touring France, Switzerland, the Rhineland, Holland and Belgium, and frequenting the theaters, cafés and salons of Paris. Here he is also reunited with Giulia Rinieri, who has married her cousin only to join her lover wherever and whenever she can. ("Giulia, who at first seemed the weakest, surpassed them all in strength of character.") In ten years he writes *Memoirs of an Egotist*, *Italian Chronicles*, *Lucien Leuwen*, *The Life of Henry Brulard*, *Memoirs of a Tourist*, *The Charterhouse of Parma*, and *Lamiel*, not to mention his voluminous correspondence, but his itinerary is still that of a student sowing wild oats. At fifty-seven he has his "Last Romance" in Rome with the Contessa Cini. A year later he suffers his first attack of apoplexy ("there is nothing wrong with dying in the street," he writes to his friend Di Fiore, "as long as one doesn't do it on purpose") but recovers for one more brief affair.

Looking out over Lake Albano toward the end of his life, he thinks that his whole history could be summed up by the initials of eleven women and "the inanities and follies they inspired me to commit." Yet those who run wild must have the strength to run: it takes an extraordinary man to have the emotional energy, the spontaneity to be childish at fifty. As he put it, "to possess a strong character one must have had an extensive experience of the disappointments and miseries of life: then one either desires constantly or not at all."

The critics who complained of Stendhal's "childishness" and "immorality" missed the source of his genius, the strength which allowed him to keep his youthful responsiveness even as he grew old and wise. When he manifests a heedless capacity for both joy and sorrow to the end of his life, he is giving us a clue to the abilities which enabled him to write the most intensely alive novels in literature. He himself understood very well the springs of his inspiration:

> After the adventures of early youth, one's heart chills to sympathy. Losing childhood's companions through death or absence, one is reduced to spending life with indifferent acquaintances, forever measuring, ruler in hand, the considerations of interest and vanity. Gradually, tenderness and generosity dry up, and before a man is thirty he finds that his gentle and loving emotions have become petrified. In the midst of this arid desert, love strikes a spring that gushes forth with fresher and more abundant feelings than those of childhood.
>
> *On Love*

Stendhal is one of those rare souls who never stopped desiring *to be alive, to be in love, to be free*. These three desires dominate his works.

However, as Balzac said, we owe Stendhal to the contrast between the North and the Mediterranean: the man who wishes to be described on his tomb as "Arrigo Beyle

Milanese" is still obsessed by French logic. In a sense the "perpetual adolescent" Beyle is but an experimental subject for the "cynic" Stendhal, who thus becomes master of both passion and irony. His childhood friend and maternal grandfather, Dr. Gagnon, never ceased to impress upon him the importance of *knowing the human heart*, and Stendhal, his magnificent pride notwithstanding, dissects his own as if it were a guinea pig. Which accounts for the difference between his personal memoirs and *Journal* and most other writers' fiction: he talks about us even when he is concerned only with himself, while they write about themselves even when portraying others. And what he learns in the laboratory of his *Journal* he applies to the world of his novels. If his main pursuit is happiness, he also knows that it is the essential pursuit of all human beings, and his characters stand out so sharply because he asks the most vital and revealing questions: what gives them joy? what is it they truly love and hate?

His first masterpiece, *On Love*, grew out of his struggle to understand his insensate passion for Mathilde Dembowski. Since it was this work which provoked most critics to call him "cold" and "a cynic," it may be instructive to record how he finished it at the age of thirty-nine:

> I went up to my charming room on the third floor and cried as I corrected the proofs of *On Love*. It's a book that I wrote with a pencil in Milan, during my lucid intervals. Working on it in Paris hurt me. I never wanted to finish it.
>
> *Memoirs of an Egotist*

On Love is the distillation of *Beylisme*, the art of keeping one's head while losing one's heart. In *Being and Nothing-*

ness, Sartre (who owes a great deal to Stendhal and little to the German philosophers he quotes at such length) cites this duality as an example of "bad faith." In fact, it is the schizoid aspect of literary genius: absolute involvement and absolute detachment.

It is also the secret of great acting. The fact that "Stendhal" (derived from the name of a Prussian town) was only one of the hundred and twenty-nine pseudonyms that Beyle invented for himself ought to discourage anyone from presuming to understand him too well. Still, his fondness for assuming different identities betrays at least one other striking ability. All writers must have something of the actor in them—to create a character is to impersonate him—but there is no doubt that Stendhal is the greatest actor even among the master novelists. In *The Life of Henry Brulard* he recalls that in his youth at Napoleon's court, he acquired many powerful enemies by unconsciously mimicking their expressions, and growing old in Civitavecchia, he often stood in front of the mirror, imitating postures and gestures which he found particularly striking. Balzac and Tolstoy portray a wider range of characters, but it is Stendhal who plays his heroes and heroines to the hilt.

> Everybody in France knows the story of Mademoiselle de Sommery, who was caught in the very act by her lover and denied it brazenly. When he protested, she cried out: "Oh, well, I can see that you no longer love me—you would rather believe your eyes than what I tell you!"

On Love argues that she is nearly right. Her outburst, quoted in the book, carries *ad absurdum* one of its main themes: we become aware only of what we wanted to know in the first place. Strictly speaking, Stendhal examines only the relationship between love and consciousness, but with such lucidity that he reveals the connection between all thoughts and emotions. *On Love* is thus the most useful commentary on the novels to come.

The wisdom of the English language designates "state of mind" as an emotional condition rather than a state of knowing—and this notion is also Stendhal's point of departure. He analyzes how our beliefs and opinions are formed by our psychological needs, how we reason to distort reality by accepting, rejecting, or twisting the facts of life to fit our inclinations. This process he calls *cristallisation:* the evidence crystallizes on the thread of feeling in a new and unrecognizable shape—like the "diamond"-encrusted bough he once saw in the salt mines of Hallein. We may think we know all about wishful thinking and emotional judgment (particularly in our opponents' views) but it is *On Love* that blows these phenomena up to their true proportions, by describing the process in its painful details and showing that each human being is subject to it: we all remake the world in the image of our feelings.

Illuminating the ways in which we willfully fool ourselves, *On Love* sold seventeen copies in the year of its publication; and Stendhal's analysis of self-deception has still to be fully appreciated. By one of the characteristic modes of "crystallization," we reject its significance by slighting it as a truism. Yet a truth seems obvious only when we understand it in the most superficial way. Facts are rarely obscure; our problem is to detect their relevance, their *meaning*. Thus, while we claim to know all about the ego's interest in our thinking, we continue to waste an inordinate amount of energy on the pretense that our beliefs, principles, opinions, our reasoning powers themselves are not in the pay of our emotions. This pretense (which is responsible for so many evils, from sexual prudery to ideological wars) is what Stendhal understood by *affectation*, a prime target of his irony and a current in the tension he creates in his novels.

Writing to Sainte-Beuve in 1834, Stendhal says: "If I meet God after my death, I'll be very surprised, but if he allows me to speak, I'll have plenty to say to him." He tells it all to his readers, and a lot of it concerns the affectations of envious malice.

Even today, when literature is serving the fashion of hysteria, presenting a crowded gallery of outsized monsters, madmen and sadists to demonstrate man's inhumanity to man, writers are curiously reticent about sheer, everyday malice. It appears to be so basic to our nature that it is forever denied. The received notion is that there is very little malice in the world, and a great deal of persecution complex. But Stendhal isn't shy about spite—he shows up the claim that "all the world loves a lover" for the brazen lie it is.

On Love advises the reader who is lucky enough to be passionately in love not to confide in his best friend, because "he is certain that if what you say is true, your pleasures are a thousand times better than *his* and make you despise him." Which is how malice is born. We hate ourselves for our miseries and suspect everyone else of hating us too, or else we simply envy the more fortunate and imagine that they look down on us because we look up to them; and so we hasten to forestall their disdain by despising them first—like the generals who advocate the "first-strike" nuclear strategy, urging their nation to be the first to drop its H-bombs, as a prudent preventive measure. *Malice is preemptive contempt.*

In *Lucien Leuwen*, Stendhal describes the mood of a group of army officers in a provincial garrison as they learn that a new lieutenant is arriving from Paris. All they know about the newcomer, Lucien, is that he is a rich banker's son and has lived in the capital; but as they are bored with their own cramped, penurious lives, they imagine Lucien will scorn them, and so they have no trouble in "seeing through him." They decide that he is overbearing, stupid, weak, and worthless before they can possibly have any notion of what sort of person he is, and they employ all the mean little tricks of army life to make him pay for his "conceit." What might have been an easy satire on provincials becomes in Stendhal's hands the analysis of a common human trait: any sign of happiness in others strikes most of us as an offense, which we feel compelled to revenge. Lucien's father has just as many enemies in the political and financial world of Paris as his son has in the provinces, because he is cheerful and witty by nature and is suspected of having unlimited wealth and influence. *Lucien Leuwen*, by the way, (unfinished in as completed a state as Schubert's *Unfinished* Symphony) is still the most up-to-date novel on modern politics and, along with *The Charterhouse of Parma*, allows the reader to discover the inspirational role that spite plays in political theories, stratagems and intrigues.

The master of irony doesn't miss out on the one-sided nature of malice. The people we envy rarely feel enviable.

The rich lieutenant Lucien, whom the other officers despise for his "arrogance," is miserable, lacks self-confidence and envies in his turn the officers who have made it in the army without their fathers' help. At the court of Parma, a careless sign of favor from the ruling monarch is enough to make the lucky courtier, Fabrizio, an object of hatred although he is so depressed that he is thinking of suicide. People don't really have to be better, better off, more intelligent, or (worst crime) happier than we are—the mere suspicion that they might be is enough to convince us of their contempt for us and inspire us to retaliate.

"There is a passionate pride in being mediocre." The phrase is Sartre's but the revelation is in Stendhal's novels. In *The Red and the Black*, Julien Sorel, a miller's son, is beaten by his father for reading books—a sign of the boy's wish to be superior. The rationalization is that he is "lazy." When Julien becomes tutor to the mayor's children and exchanges his peasant jacket for a smart black suit, his own brothers ambush him in the woods and leave him lying in his blood for the tailor's art. In Stendhal's world, as in ours, most people have a greater interest in beating down others than in bettering themselves.

The spitefulness of the Stendhalian characters depends not on their fixed "character" but on their emotional state. Julien Sorel (who suffers as much from a persecution complex as from the real spite he's subjected to) is finally condemned to death because he refuses to humble himself before the jury, and yet he is capable of despising his devoted mistress, Mme de Rênal, as an empty and selfish woman, whenever he suspects her of pride.

On every page of Stendhal's novels, the characters are ready to change their attitudes toward people, to persuade themselves of new and "impartial" judgments and act upon them, at the moment their ego is wounded.

It must be emphasized that none of this is on a complaining note: the gasping self-pity which turns most books on the human condition into nauseating revelations of the authors' deep sorrow for themselves is alien to Stendhal's realism. Far from sentimentalizing his characters' misery, he shows it as the chief inspiration for evil. He is teaching the reader to beware of himself, *beware of the unhappy*.

We may become virtuous (or at any rate harmless to ourselves and others) if we are truly happy, for contentment is a generous and even humble state of mind. This is the importance of love—yet love, too, has its rationalizations.

Mme de Rênal grew up in a convent and has no thoughts or desires other than the ones her education allows her to have. Submissive and timid, sincerely devout, she is a faithful wife and a loving mother; she is also a snob, a provincial *bourgeoise* who dutifully detests Napoleon (Julien's secret hero) and is held up by all the petty tyrants of the small town as an example to their wives. Until the arrival of Julien in her household, the word *amour* means nothing to her but vile, revolting debauchery. When she falls in love with him, she can explain her sentiments: she is overjoyed that her children have a kind tutor who doesn't beat them, she feels sorry for this poor miller's son, she is concerned with his well-being out of Christian charity. And so she is "perfectly happy, thinking of nothing but Julien, without the slightest notion of reproaching herself." When she can no longer remain unaware of her love, she admits it to herself by disclaiming it: "This fit of madness will pass."

She is relieved that she has nothing to fear. It is by such twists of consciousness that she finally becomes his mistress.

Julien, for his part, inflamed by ambition, has firm and considered opinions about the worthlessness of all other emotions. He prides himself so much on his rationality that while he is head over heels in love with Mme de Rênal, he still pretends to himself that he is playing with her.

Affectations like these produce the charming ironies in our lives, but the irony is in a contradiction that can grow to ruin us. When Julien leaves her, Mme de Rênal convinces herself that the void left by his absence is *remorse*, guilt, proof of her sin; and when she is asked for a character reference to pave the way for his marriage to the daughter of a marquis, she is persuaded that she owes it "to the sacred cause of religion and morality" to write a letter that will cut off both his marriage and his career. Julien, resolved to act and speak only to get ahead, doesn't realize his passion for Mme de Rênal until (a fanatical believer in calculating every move) he rushes back to Verrières and tries to kill her.

In short, no naïve rationalist could be pleased with Stendhal. If you appreciate yourself for your opinions and principles, if you think they place you above less high-minded people, he isn't your author. None of his books can be read without acquiring the uneasy feeling that we know nothing of a person if we only know his views. He is the novelist who puts ideas and ideologies in their place: if they are relevant to the character, they are expressions of an inner condition; if not, they are meaningless—or worse, they are poison.

But what of the feelings that lead us to false ideas? Stendhal isn't party to the kind of cynicism with which we protect ourselves from involvement. People are ever ready, he notes in *On Love*, to ridicule the madness of all absorbing interests, in order to encourage themselves to have none. The affectation that wisdom lies in the absence of emotion is inspired by the most contemptible emotion of all, the dread of feeling, which leads us to what he calls (in English) the *dead blank*.

We cannot escape from the domination of our psychological state, the only question is which emotions will master our being. This is from *On Love*:

> While the zealous nobody is consumed by boredom, avarice, hate and all the icy and bitter passions, I spend a cheerful night dreaming of her.

As both capitalist and communist states—not to mention the technological world—have evolved under the illusion that men purposefully built them, ideological optimism seeps into every niche of our lives. It is made worse by mass culture which feeds our most destructive illusions, fostering the belief that if we're only justified (and who isn't?)—if we only calculate things correctly, if we only *do the right thing* (and who doesn't?)—then the future must yield the desired results. There must always be a way. And so hubris turns hopes to false certainties, everyone expects to be a winner, and each tomorrow is a mind-blowing surprise.

Which is why we need Stendhal more than perhaps any other generation: his novels show us how tomorrow works. Tolstoy wrote the best study on the tenuous connection between men's aims and life's results, but it is Stendhal who exposes at every turn the fundamental condition of our lives. Chaos is his specialty.

There is, to begin with, his understanding of the chaotic

contradictions within each character. We cannot count on people to act in the way they have led us to believe they always would. The provincial prefect in *Lucien Leuwen* risks losing his job and his chances of advancement, the fruits of long years of shameless servility, by throwing the by-election to the opposition candidate, in a sudden fit of wounded vanity. Lucien's father, the rich Parisian banker who acts and talks like the prototype of the successful capitalist and believes in nothing but money and power, in fact has so little interest in either that, to everyone's surprise, he dies a poor man.

Irving Howe pays Stendhal a misleading compliment when he praises the extreme political sophistication of *The Charterhouse of Parma* because the head of the liberal opposition party in the principality, Fabio Conti, is also the despot's craven prison governor, ever ready to connive in the murder of Ernesto IV's victims. Stendhal is much more sophisticated than that. Seeing through the transparent dissimulations of power politics is child's play compared with his accomplishment in describing the true relationship in each of his characters' consciousness between their ideas, principles or intentions and their real nature.

The result shows society in a light that makes the image of a neat and tidy world of oppression (where even treacherous liberals pursue basely but simply their self-interest) look like just another daydream, an altogether too orderly and rational nightmare. *The Charterhouse of Parma* reveals modern totalitarianism operating under the same old non-rules as the Wars of the Roses. If the liberal prison governor is ready to sacrifice Fabrizio's life to the Prince's spite (and his own), it is Conte Mosca, the Prince's avowedly opportunistic and efficiently ruthless prime minister, who

(177)

organizes the prisoner's escape. (*"Here I am, committing high treason," the Conte said to himself, wild with joy.*) One cannot even rely on politicians to be consistently vile, any more than one can count on them to keep faith with their noble speeches.

Beyond the darkness that descended on Europe with the victory of the Holy Alliance, there is the darker world of unpredictability.

Stendhal doesn't only suggest this, he proves it. His heroes and heroines are armed with all the best weapons against the world and exploit to the full every conceivable opportunity to achieve their aims. They do not fail, they are defeated.

Julien Sorel, the commoner determined to get to the top, is a near-genius. At the age of fourteen he has the wit to recognize from a single trivial incident the fact that in post-Napoleonic France a peasant boy cannot hope to rise in the red coat of the army, that the only way up is in the black cassock of the church.

> All at once, Julien stopped talking about Napoleon; he announced his intention of becoming a priest and was constantly to be seen in his father's sawmill, memorizing a Latin Bible that the curé had lent him. This good old man, marveling at his progress, spent whole evenings teaching him theology. In his company, Julien expressed nothing but pious sentiments. Who could have guessed that this pale, gentle, girlish face concealed the unshakable determination to risk a thousand deaths rather than fail to make his fortune?

Determination, self-denial, intelligence, imagination, dreams of glory—and a series of lucky and unlucky accidents—carry him from the sawmill to the Rênal household to the seminary at Besançon to the Hôtel de La Mole in Paris, as private secretary to a powerful aristocrat. For all his calculations, he is trustworthy and loyal, as well as efficient, and is soon entrusted with all the Marquis de La Mole's business affairs and dangerous political intrigues, handling them better than the Marquis himself, who wishes that his son could be more like Julien. When the "monstrously proud" Mathilde de La Mole falls in love with him and invites him to her room at midnight, he suspects a trap: he is convinced that the young noblemen want to kill him and are planning an ambush; yet he keeps the date, pistols in hand. He wouldn't excuse himself if he were careless, he never wants to say "I didn't think of that." He always thinks of *everything*. Even the things he doesn't calculate work to his advantage: when Mathilde becomes pregnant she insists on marrying him, and the enraged Marquis is eventually forced to set about turning his secretary into an aristocrat. Julien becomes the Chevalier de La Vernaye, Lieutenant of Hussars, stationed at Strasbourg with his horses, his uniforms, his liveried servants. He is intoxicated with ambition.

> . . . he was already calculating that he would have to be more than a mere lieutenant at twenty-three in order to be commander-in-chief by thirty at the latest, like all the great generals. He thought of nothing but glory and his son.

At this moment, the Marquis has already received the letter of denunciation from Mme de Rênal.

The significance of her letter is that it brings Julien to realize what has mattered most to him in life. The realization comes to him too late, this is his tragedy. But as far as his social ambitions are concerned, he has done everything humanly possible. He was found wanting in nothing, no one could have done things better. Yet in truth even his temporary successes are due rather to accident than to his calculations and efforts, and in the end he is beaten.

Had Julien been any less willing or capable, his story would have been inconclusive. Indeed, literature is crowded with the misfortunes of weak or obsessed characters who are overwhelmed by life, leaving both themselves and the reader *at a loss*. Such characters—even as conceived by a Dostoevski or a Kafka—may be moving and convincing but their very helplessness limits their relevance: one can never be certain that a saner or stronger man would not have done better in their place. The limits of the human condition haven't been tested. We're left with a bewildering sense of the "mystery" of life, which can exercise our compassion and feed our self-pity, but which adds little to our understanding of the rules of existence.

Stendhal has no use for the art of the inconclusive. After his first novel, *Armance*, he discarded half-hearted characters who could not probe the ultimate limits of passion, will and capability. Although he condemned Napoleon for "robbing France of her liberties," he never ceased to be a fascinated admirer of the intelligence, energy, ingenuity, courage and determination that allowed a Corsican nobody to become an emperor. Like Tolstoy after him, he saw Napoleon as the definitive *doer*, the explorer of the possibilities of human mastery over events. And so he creates Napoleonic characters. Julien often compares himself to the young Bonaparte, and the comparison is justified by his talents and actions. There is no "mystery of life" in the Stendhal novel: whatever his central characters are trying to do, the reader can take it at the end that the thing *has been tried*.

Even such a spirited woman as Anna Karenina compares unfavorably with one of Stendhal's least strong-willed heroines, Mme de Rênal. She is timid and can be bullied by her pious notions into ruining Julien and herself, but her failure is in misunderstanding what happens to her, not in weakness of character. After Julien's attempt on her life, she doesn't hesitate to expose herself to ridicule and condemnation in a public effort to save him. She *thinks* of suicide but she carries on until her heart stops beating.

However, no character, male or female, can compare with Gina Sanseverina of *The Charterhouse of Parma*. There is nothing in the world she doesn't know: she understands men, she understands politics, she knows how to charm, she knows how to fight. This woman is never deceived by false notions: she even knows herself. She is also highborn, rich and powerful. Conte Mosca, the prime minister of Parma and a profound master of diplomacy and intrigue, is her slave. Without even trying, she can inspire passions that lead men to risk their lives and commit murder to please her. It has been noted that she makes even literary critics lose their heads; to quote only Balzac, she is "frank, naïve, sublime, submissive, spiritual, passionate . . . she embodies the genius of Italy." There has never been a real or imaginary human being so well equipped to get what she wanted from life—or who wanted it so badly. "The universe is a footpath to her passion." She wants her nephew. Everything she does, she does for Fabrizio. He has the most sincere affection and admiration for her, but he has fallen in love with someone else, and there isn't a thing that she can do about it.

Her love rejected, her life in danger, she hears loud voices in the house at midnight:

> "Good!" she thought, "they're coming to arrest me. So much the better. That will give me something to do, fighting them for my head."

The Duchessa Sanseverina not only illuminates the impossibility of controlling our destiny, she can even reconcile us to it.

Readers who have yawned through one too many "serious" novels need not keep their distance from Stendhal. His works are not displays of ponderous fatuity, devised to prove how deep the author's mind is and how difficult his craft. They are not the sort of books that are trumpeted by the culture phonies who dictate literary opinion in every age and every country and who are unfailingly opposed to art—perhaps for the simple reason that they are chiefly interested in art, while art is chiefly interested in life. Such people can easily live with falsehood because they are horrified of nothing but vulgarity—that is, reality without the cushioning of affectation. They considered Stendhal cheap, vulgar and "inartistic" in his time and even today they cannot write of his works without condescension. Stendhal is too lively for them, even in the grave.

This needs saying because Stendhal's dedication "to the happy few" has been picked up by these precious few as a slogan of their caste. He detested these bookish "halfwits whose vanity compels them to talk about literature and make a pretense of thinking," and it was primarily their mob that he meant to exclude from the happy circle of his readers (which he hoped would contain "beings such as

Mme Roland and M. Gros, the geometrician"—his old mathematics teacher in Grenoble). In his day they praised and admired writers who are now completely forgotten or still remembered for their monumental achievements in melodramatic absurdity, tortured psychology and unnatural style—Chateaubriand, Alfred de Vigny, Fenimore Cooper, Walter Scott. They considered Stendhal's novels literally beneath contempt and denied themselves the satisfaction of attacking him in print for fear that even negative reviews might encourage some perverse reader to buy his books. *The Charterhouse of Parma* received one single review (a favor from the *Revue de Paris* to Stendhal as one of its contributors) in the year of its publication—an outrage which finally prompted Balzac to set down his seventy-two-page *Etudes sur M. Beyle*, "in admiration, compelled by conscience."

However, Balzac, of all people, couldn't help noting that M. Beyle was "very fat" and (while spelling his subject's pen name "Stendahl") castigated him for "negligent errors" of grammar and style—concluding with the suggestion that he should polish his manuscript to achieve the poetic perfection of Chateaubriand. No wonder Stendhal took two weeks to compose his thank-you note, grateful though he was for Balzac's many true insights. The three drafts of his answer give us some idea why he is above all *a good read*. "I've been told," he wrote to Balzac, "that I should give the reader a rest from time to time by describing landscape, clothes, etc. Those things have bored me so much in other books!" He wouldn't inflict on his readers the sort of "obligatory" passages he himself found tiresome—which is why he is one of the few authors we can read without skipping. Excusing his negligent errors on the grounds that the book was dictated in just over nine weeks, he confided innocently that he had never thought of the *art* of writing a novel and had no idea that there were rules about it. As for what Balzac had called "that character of perfection, the seal of irreproachable beauty which Chateaubriand and de Maistre gave to their beloved books"—

> While I was writing *The Charterhouse*, I sometimes read a few pages of the Civil Code in order to catch the right tone. . . . I could never read twenty pages of M. de Chateaubriand; I almost had to fight a duel because I made fun of "the indeterminate crest of the forests" . . . I find M. de Maistre insupportable. No doubt that's why I write badly—from an exaggerated love of logic.

He confessed that he knew of only one rule in writing: *to be clear.* ("I often reflect for a quarter of an hour whether to put an adjective before or after a noun. I try to recount (1) truthfully, (2) clearly, what goes on in a human heart.") Out of gratitude for Balzac's enthusiastic review, he made the (unkept) promise to "improve" his language; but there was no doubt in his mind about who was right. As he had already written elsewhere: "Only a profound mind would dare a straight style. That's why Rousseau put so much rhetoric into *La Nouvelle Héloïse.*"

Unappreciated by his contemporaries, he wrote for future generations, and this has a direct bearing on the fact that his masterpieces have the pace, economy and tension of good thrillers. Assuming that his future readers would neither know nor care about the period he lived in, he found it easy to ignore the great ephemeral issues of his time, the sort of front-page problems that find their way into most books and date them in a few decades, if not a couple of months. His novels include nothing which is not of the utmost significance to the characters or their story. Balzac, who spoiled some of his own works by excessive documentation of the purely temporary, identified Conte Mosca of *The Charterhouse of Parma* with Count Metternich; Stendhal's response to the suggestion was cool:

> I had no intention of portraying M. de Metternich . . . I dream of having some little success around 1860 or 1880. By then there will be very little talk of M. de Metternich . . . Death makes us exchange roles with such people.

Stendhal isn't for scholars or the luckily limited number of literary intellectuals: his theme is the human emotions we all share. He doesn't count on pleasing pretentious women or "practical" men who are too busy making a hundred thousand francs a year and meeting a weekly payroll of two thousand workers to *waste their time* on anything but useful facts, nor the student who is "so delighted with having learned modern Greek that he's already thinking of taking up Arabic"; but he doesn't exclude from his happy few the sort of people who strike it rich on the Bourse or in a lottery. Such emotion-stirring gambles, he thinks, are quite compatible with the feelings inspired by a great painting, a phrase of Mozart's or a look in a woman's eyes.

As Balzac said, Stendhal can be read "with bated breath, craning neck, goggling eyes, by anyone who has an imagination, or even just a heart."

Writers who stuff their readers with the most preposterous lies, appearing more ignorant of real life than one would have thought possible, are usually called romantics.

(*185*)

It's a nice and reputable word, as if believing in a lot of nonsense were a harmless and even perhaps admirable pastime. The adjective "romantic" has also been applied to Stendhal, with absolutely no justification, by dried-up critics who are shocked by the very idea that men and women can be possessed by feelings. Those who call him a cynic and complain that he robs us of our illusions are at least stating a fact.

We live in a haze of illusions, never quite certain who we are or where we are, suffering "anxiety neurosis" and "crisis of identity." When Stendhal robs us of our false notions about love, reason, action and history, he clears away the haze and allows us to touch ground. "This is life," the reader can say, "this is what it means to be a human being, this is what I must cope with."

Freeing life from its lies, he also communicates its *force*, which fills our senses, our emotions, our impulses, but which we learn to betray.

Most of our adult life is spent in little compromises which enable us to get along with other human beings but also reduce our feeling of individuality, our sense of our own uniqueness and importance. We're keenly aware—more so perhaps in this age of overpopulation and mass communication than ever before—that each one of us is a superfluous nonentity in the scheme of things. This makes it easier for others to handle us and more difficult for us to handle ourselves—which is why all tyrannies make humility the greatest virtue. This virtue, this servility, this denial of self which is euphemistically called "conformism," even swamps our will to live.

The mainspring of all Stendhal's work is the emotional tension between our immediate impulses, our true feelings, and the pressure to check them for the sake of our social role. In this tension we often warp and even exchange our living self for a kind of functioning machine. This is Julien Sorel's keenest torment: his own powerful impulses conflicting with what he conceives as the necessity to make all his words and gestures conform to an expected and supposedly successful pattern. But this problem isn't confined to the underdog and outsider: Lucien Leuwen, the rich boy, feels it just as keenly, as does Fabrizio del Dongo, the Italian aristocrat.

For the impulsive, passionate, "childish" Stendhal, it was the problem of his life—spending as he did many years in the army, at court, in the diplomatic service (not to mention the all-important literary salons), where every look, every gesture, every word had its consequences—and facing even worse hazards in the constant company of the women he worshiped and so desperately wanted to please. To adjust or to be oneself—this is the drama that is always there, in every moment that we spend with others. Stendhal had to face it also as a writer: should he or shouldn't he play literary politics? should he or shouldn't he apply the "poetic" style? As Valéry wrote, "he was divided between his great desire to please and to achieve glory and the *mania*, the *sensual pleasure*, of being himself. . . ."

Julien Sorel, condemned to the guillotine for the attempted murder of Mme de Rênal, is offered the chance of a pardon if he will only publicly repent his sin and undergo a religious conversion. However, this young man, this most cynical opportunist who prided himself on never uttering a word in earnest, has come to realize that we can depend on absolutely nothing in this world, neither on hopes realized nor hopes thwarted—that we're rich or poor, defeated or victorious only in the way we feel about ourselves, and therefore nothing is worth so much as this feeling, the only thing we truly possess. And so he refuses to *pretend* any more, even to save his life. *"And what would I have left,"* *Julien answered coldly, "if I despised myself?"*

The sensual joy that inspires Julien's decision is the Stendhalian beat, striking in the reader's own soul "that which is fierce, jealous, and incommunicable." No one can read Stendhal and feel redundant or altogether beaten. He rekindles our pride.

Victory of Samothrace, Louvre, Paris (CULVER PICTURES, INC.)

Rule Number Five

ONLY THE DEFEATED SURVIVE

I

ALL MEN are powerless against chance, but the defeated know the secret. They live for the present—the future has already betrayed them. They are the children of reality.

I I

THE CARTESIAN "I think, therefore I am" is a very limited insight. The question is, *who* are we? We are all subject to a bewildering flux of thoughts and feelings, which offer no clue to our character unless we act upon them.

This is most strikingly evident in our sexual lives. The strength of a woman's libido doesn't define her as a sexual being: she may turn out to be a lusty Lesbian or a hot-blooded onanist, and she may equally well be a female Don Juan or a passionate wife. She reveals herself only when she does something about her heartbeat.

And what is a man's lust without the act of erection? At one time or another I suppose every man has tried to convince a doubtfully waiting woman that he wanted her more than life, with a burning passion, even if it was palpably too feeble to prompt an erection. Such awkward moments show with devastating clarity how questionable are all feelings and designs which fail to manifest themselves in action.

As a man's body measures his desires with exactitude, no one has ever talked about the "mysterious male." There is nothing enigmatic about him—it can easily be seen whether he is ready for a woman or not. The woman, however, cannot even judge for herself the force of her passion. As it cannot manifest itself in the act of erection, it is subject to substitution, self-deception, and pretense.

At a party in Chelsea the other day I overheard one mysterious woman saying to another: "If I had to have an erection every time I made love with my husband he'd have murdered me years ago."

I I I

ONLY ACTION can testify to the validity of thoughts and emotions: action alone verifies the personality. It is the only authentic form of self-expression: *I act, therefore I know who I am.*

I V

THE VICTORS are schemers, corrupted by their luck. They look upon action as a paper currency, neither good nor bad, worthless in itself, its value lying solely in the result it is supposed to be exchanged for. They forsake rational and moral consideration of their actions in favor of estimating the rewards—which, more often than not, fail to materialize. They are like the gambler who has won a fortune at roulette and no longer counts the money he puts on the table, but only the winnings to come.

By REFUSING to acknowledge that events occur independently of his will, the successful pragmatist betrays not only external reality but his own being. When he suppresses his primary response to a course of action for the sake of some future end, he denies himself the opportunity to find out who he is. He depersonalizes what he's actually doing and personalizes his aims, which belong to dreamland; and so his personality itself acquires the uncertainty of a dream. His acts no longer mirror him, or rather he doesn't know whether they do or not: it may be that his "suppressed" preferences were too feeble to require much suppressing. In any case, the direct relationship between his personality and his life is broken: there is a gap, a void of doubt, to be filled by neurotic anxieties and obsessions. He no longer quite knows who he is; he is losing himself.

In *Division Street: America*, Studs Terkel encounters a successful Chicago salesman who clinches sales by acquiring the opinions of his customers, until he no longer knows what he himself is thinking. The man says:

> "Eventually you come to the point where you have to psychoanalyze yourself and find out, 'Why am I thinking this particular way? Is it because I'm going to make another sale tomorrow?' "

"Surely my actions don't reflect on me?" the assassin asks wistfully. "My actions are external and neutral—if you want to know what *I* am like, you must consider my feelings, my ideals, my intentions. Don't watch what I'm doing, think of what is inside my head."

But murder and mass murder are only the samples in the

window of the shop: inside there are all the little acts which we gamble for the imagined winnings, acts toward which we are indifferent or positively hostile, and which give us a distorted reflection of our personality. We are like the girl who never had a chance to look into a mirror and could only study her blurred and elongated image in the back of a spoon. Thus we can never know what we are really like and we live in dread of ourselves.

V I

THOSE WHO have nothing to look forward to have no temptation to betray their senses, their instincts, impulses, ideas or principles, and so their actions can express their identity. They may not know much, but they have some notion of what sort of characters they are, and this is strength. Authenticity is the virtue of the defeated.

Yet where is one to draw the line between the authentic and the just plain stupid? Are we to put our hands into fire without thought of the consequences? There are relatively few obvious choices like that, but the defeated learn to judge particular chances through the wise habit of living in the present. Having a firmer hold on themselves, they find it easier to accept that they have no hold over destiny, that success is good luck and failure is misfortune. Willing to try anything once, they may be more adventurous than "practical" men; but they're unlikely to persist in any enterprise if the course of events is against it. They can "roll with the punches."

Without these virtues it would be impossible to account for the survival of persecuted communities throughout the ages.

IT IS a joy to have nothing to lose and nothing to gain, as Stendhal often observed in connection with the Italian art of living. Oppressed by the Austrians and the Church and having few opportunities to improve their lot, the Milanesi of his day lived primarily to please themselves. They could afford the luxury of their emotions.

> The Milanese is not malicious, and he assures you of this with the only valid guarantee: *he is happy*. This much is self-evident, the explanation is hypothetical.
>
> Out of every hundred and fifty actions, significant or insignificant, great or small, which go to make up a day of his life, the Milanese performs a hundred and twenty solely because they appeal to him *at the moment*.
>
> He acts against his immediate inclinations, out of *sense of duty* sanctioned by the misery he would incur by doing otherwise, no more than thirty times.
>
> Out of a hundred and fifty actions which make up an Englishman's day, he performs a hundred and forty solely because it is his *duty*, sanctioned by the fear of hell as preached by Mr. Irving or by the fear of scorn if his coat isn't quite up to the fashion. I'm convinced that more than one English peer or millionaire is afraid to cross his legs when he's sitting by himself in front of his fire, for fear of being *vulgar*.
>
> . . . Not one Englishman in a hundred has the courage to be himself; not one Italian in ten could conceive the possibility of being otherwise. An Englishman is moved about once a month—an Italian, three times a day.
>
> Stendhal: *Rome, Naples and Florence*

Another foreign observer, Joseph Heller, chooses a venerable Italian as the representative of carefree common sense in *Catch-22*. The old man argues with Nately, an American airman, in the zany comfort of a Rome brothel, shortly before the end of World War II.

"America," he said, "will lose the war. And Italy will win it."

"America is the strongest and most prosperous nation on earth," Nately informed him with lofty fervor and dignity. "And the American fighting man is second to none."

"Exactly," agreed the old man pleasantly, with a hint of taunting amusement. "Italy, on the other hand, is one of the least prosperous nations on earth. And the Italian fighting man is probably second to all. And that's exactly why my country is doing so well in this war while your country is doing so poorly."

Nately guffawed with surprise, then blushed apologetically for his impoliteness. "I'm sorry I laughed at you," he said sincerely, and he continued in a tone of respectful condescension. "But Italy was occupied by the Germans and is now being occupied by us. You don't call that doing very well, do you?"

"But of course I do," exclaimed the old man cheerfully. "The Germans are being driven out, and we are still here. In a few years you will be gone, too, and we will still be here. You see, Italy is really a very poor and weak country, and that's what makes us so strong. Italian soldiers are not dying any more. But American and German soldiers are. I call that doing extremely well. Yes, I am quite certain that Italy will survive this war and still be in existence long after your own country has been destroyed."

Nately could scarcely believe his ears. He had never heard such shocking blasphemies before . . .

"I don't believe anything you tell me," Nately replied, with a bashful mitigating smile. "The only thing I do believe is that America is going to win the war."

"You put so much stock in *winning wars*," the grubby iniquitous old man scoffed. "The real trick lies in *losing* wars, in knowing which wars can be *lost*. Italy has been losing wars for centuries, and just see how splendidly we've done nonetheless. France wins wars and is in a continual state of crisis. Germany loses and prospers. Look at our own recent history. Italy won a war in Ethiopia and promptly stumbled into serious trouble. Victory gave us such insane delusions of grandeur that we helped start a world war we hadn't a chance of winning. But now that we are losing again, everything has taken a turn for the better, and we will certainly come out on top again if we succeed in being defeated."

Nately gaped at him in undisguised befuddlement. "Now I really don't understand what you're saying. You talk like a madman."

"But I live like a sane one. . . ."

The old man proves his point by reminding the American that he has survived for a hundred and seven years.

V I I I

DON JUAN, too, should be counted among the defeated. He knows it's all up to the woman and there isn't much he can do about it. Paradoxically, or perhaps not so paradoxically at all, it is his defeatism which accounts for his success. Since he has no faith in the effectiveness of his charm, he uses his daring and skill to test his chances, not to persist where he isn't wanted.

"Son," a contented old lecher once told me, "I've tried my luck under every skirt, but I've never tried to rip one off."

Don Juan demonstrates, in his own merry way, Sartre's stern dictum that "life begins beyond despair."

I X

THE DESPAIR of the rebel is not so amusing. When the defeated cease to care not only about tomorrow but even about today, death becomes their best friend.

"Shoot me!" "Kill me!" rioting blacks taunted the National Guardsmen defending the White House, the day after Martin Luther King was murdered. They only played with the notion, not quite ready, satisfied with burning their slums and looting shops—still hopeful that a free TV set or a new pair of shoes might make all the difference. It is when they no longer wish for anything that they will be ready to kill or be killed.

Colonel Adekunle of the Federal Nigerian Army told *The Observer* in the fall of 1968: "There is no hope of the rebels surrendering. They appear to want to die."

X

MAY THIS writer use his experience as a rebel against communist tyranny to comment on the spirit of Resistance fighters, Vietcong guerrillas, Latin American revolutionaries, Biafran rebels, insurrectionists everywhere? We're unlikely to share many ideas, but then rebellion has little to do with ideas, it's a sense of freezing air around the heart, a desperate conviction that (as Camus put it) *the way things are, life is not worth living.*

I reached such a pitch of absolute and malevolent despair in Budapest on 23 October 1956. At over a decade's distance, it's difficult for me to tell the scene apart from all the shouting and shooting tumults I've watched since then on television. Still, there's the memory of a big, ugly modern building, an arsenal of ghosts (much like the Los Angeles City Hall) and a huge expanse of flat concrete suddenly filling with thousands of people, swarming around a fifteen- or twenty-ton lie in bronze, the statue of Stalin, already denounced by the Twentieth Party Congress but still towering there, a willful and spiteful insult.

We were revolted, but not yet in revolt: we were content to pull down the statue and shout and push against each other for a better world, for *some* concession from those in power, and then cry victory and go home. That evening I had a date with my wife for a movie at nine o'clock; I assumed that by then it would be all over and done with. I arrived a month late.

After the statue came down at 9:30 in the evening and as our voices were getting hoarse with celebration, we heard the muffled but rapid, rhythmic knocks of submachine guns from several blocks away: the security police were mowing down the demonstrators at the Broadcasting Building. The huge Stalin Square was dark but for a few spotlights and torches, not enough to light the grounds; I could sense rather than see the people around me. The crowd grew quiet, listening to that peculiar staccato, which after a while suddenly ceased. For a few seconds or minutes there was a total silence. No, you could hear the breathing of several thousand people in chorus—it's a sound to twist your stomach. Then there was a murmur, incoherent but unmistakable—we all seemed to know what it meant. It said: "Things can't go on like that, we don't want to live like dogs, kicked or shot at whenever they feel like it." To swallow the sound of those submachine guns was too high a price for life. We saw blood even before we reached the bleeding corpses on the sidewalk in front of the Broadcasting Building, and when I heard somebody shout that the soldiers were giving away arms, I ran after him. During the weeks of the fighting (not counting the few days before Suez when we thought we had won) I never fought or met anyone who fought for victory: I met only people who wanted to kill as many sons of bitches as they could before they got killed themselves.

There was only one question that concerned us at the time. It looks preposterous on paper, but those overwhelmed with despair know no other question: is there any reason why we shouldn't die? And as long as the answer was *no*, we felt compelled to kill. If we had to die, we wanted to make sure that those who obliterated our reasons for living would go before us—the Indians' notion of taking the enemy with them to be used as servants in the great beyond seems to express a universal need.

But then despair, too, is a mood that can pass. Our group fought on for nearly a month, by which time we had lost enough comrades and gained back enough of our self-respect to be alive again to rational reflection. The continued fighting brought only more destruction of the city, more death and misery, and there were other alternatives—going back to our families and neighborhoods (hoping that no stool pigeon would identify us) or trying to escape to the West. The day I saw the six-hundred-year-old Royal Library catch fire, I went home, said good-bye to my mother and nieces, and took off with my wife toward Austria, to discover new reasons for living. Still, it was a difficult decision, and I have no doubt that had we returned to find our families killed by bombs or burned by napalm few of us would have seen the point in giving up the fight.

X I

THE REBEL is a suicidal killer.

X I I

THE AMERICANS began to defeat themselves in Vietnam when they started to punish. The peasant who joined the Vietcong because he had seen more white men in his country than he could stand without self-contempt, might have had second thoughts as soon as he had fought long enough to regain his pride and love of living. There was his family, the rice field, the village to tempt him back to life, to compromise. But when the hut, the family, the fields were burned, what was the Vietcong to do but go on fighting? Imagine yourself returning home and finding only corpses and cinders. Would this persuade you to stop trying to kill those who had destroyed all you had—or for that matter, anybody you could aim at who wasn't your comrade-in-vengeance?

Yet what else could the American army do, fighting to maintain the status quo? They leave the villages alone: the

Vietcong is assured of supply and new recruits. They destroy the villages: the Vietcong fight all the more bitterly, having nowhere to retreat. The weakness of the American position has been the existential weakness of the powerful in every revolutionary situation. Having already won power, they aim to keep it: by the logic of their position, they are result-oriented. This puts them at a grave disadvantage against the defeated, who revolt against their present misery and fight for the sake of killing. It is easy to miss the point, the true inspiration of the troops, for the rebel leaders, like all leaders, belong to the other camp, among those obsessed with the future. (How else would they have become leaders?)

But even if the point isn't missed, what can the powerful do? Committed to keep what they hold, they can have no other motive: they fight to carry their prestige and power intact into the future. So their guns, their warships, their bombs have only one message: *you cannot win*. But this only deepens the rebels' despair—which drove them to fight in the first place.

It is doubtful whether it would have been possible to secure a pro-white regime in Vietnam in any case, given the country's recent history, but the opportunity may not yet have been lost in the simmering cities of the United States or on the battlefield of the generations. The only chance for the powerful is to provide reasons for living: to look and create instead of search and destroy. The show of force may intimidate demonstrators, protesters, rioters, but not rebels. It is absolutely useless to show them that they cannot win and will get killed, as they're not going to rise unless they've already decided to die. As for relying on superior weaponry to exterminate them, this is again to ignore the experience of Vietnam. A relatively small number of snipers and saboteurs can bring a country to a standstill without showing their faces; and even if most of them get caught and imprisoned or killed, who can tell at what point punishments and reprisals will push thousands of others beyond the desire to live?

X I I I

THIS IS what Zarathustra would say today to the powerful:

Hearken to my words—the rebel is mortal, but he is unconquerable—unless you vanquish his despair!

Take no pride in your firepower!

Despair cannot be conquered by vanity! Verily, men without hope are stronger than men possessed by fear.

I say unto you: there is no way to defeat those who have already been defeated!

X I V

THE EXECUTIVE raises his index finger and presses, ever so slightly, a button. A secretary appears. The Executive is confirmed in his delusion that intention-action-result are directly related in life. Of course, it's all chance's doing: the secretary might have had to go to the washroom, might have walked out to the corridor to show a stranger the way to another office, might have rushed home in a panic, without telling anyone, because her child got hurt—or some fault might have developed in the intercom system. The possibilities that could have prevented the secretary's appearance are innumerable. And now and then one of these possibilities does assert itself and the secretary doesn't spring into the inner office when the index finger exerts its slight pressure. These are the Executive's chances to learn the true nature of life, but he confuses frequency and infrequency with relevance and irrelevance: he believes that the secretary's failures to appear are of no significance because they occur so seldom, and is convinced that there is magic in his index finger when it touches a button during working hours.

The powerful, assuming that they can cause events, fail to grasp how they relate to events—and consequently fail to comprehend how others relate to events. On account of the appearing secretaries, they are as defenseless in the world as the deaf and blind.

The industrialists' blindness to the effect of advertising is characteristic of all men in power. They intended advertising to stimulate sales, production, profit, the gross national product, etc.; and it worked, especially after television came in. But after a few years, the poor-but-in-television began to be taunted by the minute-by-minute cajolery to buy all the luxury items they couldn't afford. So advertising, the erstwhile instrument of profit and stability, turned into an agent of discontent, disorder, riot, looting and hell-raising, tearing apart the system which had been so kind to the commodity kings. During the riots of the last few years, this has become a truism: television advertising succeeds where the communist party failed. Everybody knows it except those who go on spending fortunes to destroy their own security and power.

The reader, in whatever country, can observe his politicians, his business leaders, his experts and authorities and find this to be true: *the powerful cannot sense the reality of the unintended.* At best, they appreciate "side effects." But "side effect" needs a new dictionary definition, for it has increasingly come to mean an activity's main effect, which, being unwilled and unforeseen, occurred unexpectedly, remained unseen and failed to be appreciated—appearing in the light of its true significance only when it was too late to do anything about it.

X V

THE POWERFUL are not only blind, they see things that aren't there. They believe in the reality of everybody else's intentions as well as their own. Everything intended is actual for them. All governments spend fortunes to snoop on their own citizens and their "enemies," seeking to know what people are feeling, thinking and planning—even though most of these feelings, thoughts, plans do not and could not possibly influence the outcome of events and it is absolutely impossible to foretell which of them will be actualized and in what form (actions bringing about results not so much opposed to what was planned for, as entirely unrelated to it). The American government, being the best-informed of everybody's intentions, appears to be the most remote from events—while the tens of thousands of FBI and CIA agents could be employed to increase U.S. security by killing rats.

The powerful try to eliminate those who *wish* them ill; in outright dictatorships, the government even suppresses disrespectful rhymes, believing them to be as potent as the Devil's spells. All oppression in fact is based on the insane superstition that history is determined by the witchcraft of the adversaries.

The powerful fight shadows and are inattentive to the real threats to their existence.

X V I

POWER GROWS not in the direction where it is needed but along the path of least resistance, into those areas where intention can be most often rewarded by results. It is easy to manufacture poison gases, it's difficult to prevent air pollution, so states manufacture poison and plague bombs. Traffic congestion presents staggering problems with no effective solution short of a ban on private automobiles, so states build supersonic airliners and rockets to the moon.

To achieve social order and stability would be to cope with life, to impose our will upon chaos; but it is *almost* possible to build a perfect filing system. The tasks power sets itself are as a rule irrelevant, the tasks it avoids relate directly to its needs. So if anything, power labors at its own destruction. Spaceships don't reconcile people to slums and traffic jams, and not even the most orderly filing system will defuse a revolution.

X V I I

I LOVE TO travel, but for the annoying and absolutely meaningless business of having to fill in a card every time one crosses a border. I couldn't count how often I've informed the Belgian, Swiss, French, Italian, British, and

American governments that I'm a male. Eventually I began to wonder—who could possibly be reading the tens of thousands, hundreds of thousands of cards which people fill in every day at ports of entry? The answer of course was, no one. Bored with my own data, I've lately got into the habit of inventing new histories for myself. I never repeat the mistake of being born in the twentieth century; my date of birth is usually B.C., though at times I favor 1783. I jot down the bare facts of my new lives dutifully, for the scrutiny of interested authority, and hand them over to policemen-immigration clerks with the open smile of a man who cares to hide nothing.

You would be surprised at the casualness of the French police as they wave on a male-female person thousands of years old whose profession is white slave trader and whose purpose in visiting the country is to sell hashish.

I always give my correct address, just in case a curious computer or official might want to get in touch with me—but so far, not a word from any of them.

X V I I I

THE GROWTH of the modern state causes an undue degree of anxiety and fear among those who care for individual liberty. When the citizens' every move is directed by law, the law by necessity ceases to influence their behavior. When every phone is tapped, the government won't have the slightest notion what people are talking about. When taxation is fully computerized, tax evasion will attain monumental proportions. When everyone's birth, marriage and death records are kept by computers, the government will have no idea of the size of the population or of population movements. It is in this sense that Marx's prophecy about the state developing toward its own disintegration appears to be coming true.

X I X

DELUSIONS BREED cowardice.

We cannot believe falsehoods in quite the same way as truths. Unless one is clinically insane, one cannot lie to oneself with absolute conviction: reality asserts a residue of doubt, and so one is afraid to put one's daydreams to the test.

The girl who believes she is so compellingly beautiful that all men will want to rape her avoids being left alone with a man. She is terrified that he might violate her tender notion of irresistibility.

The psychological basis of such modesty is in no way different from the cowardice of the anti-Semite who believes that Jews are weaklings but wouldn't look for a Jew to fight, only for a Jew to mob. He isn't necessarily afraid of getting hurt (he may get into nasty fistfights with his friends) but he is mortally afraid that his prejudices might be wounded.

"The beauty of murder," says Nero, "is that it destroys the evidence." He points to one of his guests. "I'm stronger than he is." Four servants grab the man who is weaker than Nero and stab him with four daggers. Nero goes on eating, convinced that he could have knocked him out with his left hook. Later in the evening, while playing the flute, he conceives the telescopic rifle and the intercontinental missile.

As we acquired the delusion of godlike power, we began to need long-range weapons.

X X

THE ANGEL of Victory is a vile ghost in disguise. She poses as a beautiful, proud, and exultant woman, beating her wings in triumph, but that's not what she really looks like. When she takes off her mask, she's hideous. Her mouth is the barrel of a gun, her belly is full of bombs, her flesh is the jelly of fear and hate, and she thinks only mad thoughts. She's so popular that she's getting careless: at times she walks about the earth without her head on. Those who have caught sight of Victory in her appalling nakedness hide themselves and pray for the coming of the Lady of Defeat, to bless and save us with her radiant smile of common sense.

Death Is a Good Start

An old man, a German Jew now living in New York, told me a few years ago, "If you have any doubts about what you should do or shouldn't do, just try to imagine how you'll feel about it when you're dying. I still trust people who want to spend their last moments without shame."

I quote this to Martha.

"Are you trying to depress me?" she asks. As you will recall, she is the tallest member of the family—seventeen, emotional, tough. She doesn't like the subject, however. "It's so *boring!*" I try to convince her that she ought to keep in mind the fact that she's going to die, because this is the only way she can have a true perspective on life. She thinks I'm morbid. "Why should I make myself miserable worrying about what I'll think when I'm dying?"

"Who said you should worry? The only ideas that make you miserable are the ones you're afraid to think about. It's the unfamiliarity that scares you, not the idea." I read her some lines by George Jonas, a poet who has apparently thought long and hard enough about death to be always in high spirits.

EXIT LINES

At present I still have
A choice of deaths,
I could, for example, die of a difficult disease
For medical science and I could
Die for a stranger who has never learned to swim.
I could also die for the Queen.
These are quite honourable deaths
But they don't appeal to me.
I think I'll die for Barbara.
Strangers are strangers
Whether they can swim or not
Barbara is a friend.
Medical science
Requires long hours, depressing nights
In hospitals, syringes and white towels
For Barbara I could die with my clothes on.
The Queen, lovely as she is,
Has no breasts to compare with Barbara's
And I have never kissed the Queen's throat.
It makes sense for me to die for Barbara.

Martha grins.

"Do you feel miserable?" I ask her.

"O God!" she says wearily, and walks away with cries of despair: "I'm going to die! I'm going to die!"

I hear her sister's voice, unconcerned but mildly curious. "What's going on?"

"Stephen says you're going to die and don't you forget it!" The door of their room slams on muffled laughter.

I guess I'm lucky that I didn't get on to the subject of suicide.

We have a friend, a teacher in a tough high school, who has a big aspirin bottle containing two hundred sleeping pills. He collected them in 1966, his first and most discouraging year of teaching, which happened also to be the year when both his parents died and his wife left him. With a hefty overdose in the medicine chest, he went on living for a while with the idea that he would pull out the next day; and his troubles, which every day he expected to eliminate in twenty-four hours, became progressively less overwhelming. After all, they were only temporary, even if he never solved them. He still keeps the pills, though—he says they help him to stay his own boss.

In Montreal I once knew a lighting technician on a television crew, or rather, I saw him every day in the studio for a couple of weeks: a tall, extremely thin man standing in the shadows behind the big lamps. I used to see his face only during coffee breaks—he had sleepy eyes, a handsome big nose and high cheekbones, and a smart red mustache. He was thirty-five, someone said, and had leukemia with less than a year to go. "More light there," "to the left!" "dim it," the director or the cameraman kept telling him.

When we got talking one day over coffee, he told me that he had a "small fortune" in life insurance and for a while had thought of borrowing on his policy for a trip around the world, to say good-bye to good old earth, but his wife had talked him out of it on account of the kids. He had two children, a boy and a girl; I didn't ask how old they were. So, he had decided to work as long as he could, what else could he do?

During one of the final rehearsals he missed a couple of

lighting cues, and there was an argument, which became so heated that the director threatened to fire him from the job. He stepped forward, his face as red as his mustache, and began to curse and shout that he would take the dispute to his union. But then, abruptly, he stopped, and a sudden wild grin split his face. "Go on, boy," he said, aiming a two thousand-watt lamp right into the director's eyes, "go on, try to scare me!"

Approach to Dallas, Texas (ELLIOTT ERWITT/MAGNUM)

Rule Number Six
YOU'RE FREE AND NOBODY
BELONGS TO YOU

WHEN YOU'RE in fever, only your own body is burning, and when you're wounded, you bleed by yourself. Each man is alone inside his skin, that foolproof insulator that separates even twins and lovers.

Yet love is the only magic that can break the spell of solitude, just as life is the only magic to break the spell of death. Miracles are strictly temporary but they do happen.

The Beatles' song "All You Need Is Love" is dead wrong. It's the other way around: all love needs is *you*. Love is courage, the daring to accept foredoomed happiness.

I REMEMBER THE summer dinners in my grandparents' courtyard when I was a boy—there were over a hundred relatives present every year, of all ages, uncles, nieces, cousins, in-laws—we all knew each other and each of us had a whole tribe to back him up.

Martha was born in London, England, her sister Mary in Gravenhurst, Ontario. They are not out of grammar school yet, but they've attended classes in New York, Los Angeles, Gravenhurst, Toronto, Florence and London. Their father lives on another continent, they live in London with their mother and stepfather, who is a Hungarian by birth and a Canadian by nationality. The girls cannot name as many as twenty of their relatives. To meet their closest friends, they must travel by plane. Still, like most of their contemporaries, they feel "tied down."

To be free, to get away, is our deepest desire until we get so far that we cannot reach out to anyone.

I I I

THERE IS a new loneliness in the modern world—the *solitude of speed*. We pass by each other on the thruways of our new freedoms.

Postscript to an Erotic Novel

THERE IS little intellectual merit in argumentative fiction, and the didactic format of *In Praise of Older Women* is used as a technical device, to provide a framework for the content. To my mind, the attempt to treat fiction as a means for direct reasoning and explicit moral judgment is both futile and deceitful: it deceives the writer into believing that he influences people's thinking when he does not, and it deceives the reader by encouraging him in his dangerous delusion that thoughts can be acquired without the trouble of thinking them and truths can be bought at the price of a book, without the disturbing personal experience of discovery.

The temptation to such folly lies in our longing to pursue immortality in this world in the form of absolute truths and values; but while this longing may be irrepressible, it envelops us in self-deception and (in literature) falsehood and boredom.

Perhaps the easiest way to approach this problem is by trying to answer the question, what makes a novel "life-like"? Why is it that a crime novel leaves us unmoved, why do the atrocities inflicted by the murderer upon his innocent victims fail to shock us—while we are shaken with indignation as we read about one crook merely shortchanging another crook, in the immortal scene between Felix Krull and Master Jean-Pierre? It would seem that a novel becomes lifelike not simply by describing life but by putting the reader in a "live" situation, in which he is compelled to exercise his judgment, guess at the meaning of an action or a gesture, and try to estimate character and circumstances with no more clues than he would have in reality. The dead print thus comes alive by bringing the reader to life, by putting him on his toes, setting him up against the literary experience so that he must hold his own. "To relax with a book" is the daydream of the nonthinker that promises no illumination.

The only explicit idea in this novel is Vajda's notion (with which I fully concur) of the superiority of mature women as mistresses. And it is only this kind of explicit statement that a novel can carry on its surface; its true insights must emerge in the reader's mind. In literature, as in life, the reality and meaning of any act cannot be *given*, only *taken*.

Thus if the moral and intellectual questions raised by the life of a philanderer are in any way significant and relevant (as they are), then moral and intellectual answers are the very things the writer ought not to provide. Here I do not mean simply theoretical reflections: as any film director could testify, there are many ways to "explain" and comment on events simply by the mood of a scene; and there is, of course, the vulgar way of manipulating the plot to teach us a lesson or at least to protect us from the unflattering or disturbing implications of what we have seen or read. To take, for example, a classic, Molière's *Don Juan*, whatever shocks us in Don Juan's pursuit of pleasure, his arguments, and the complaisant behavior of his women is canceled out by his final punishment; the realities of his way of life need not worry us by their implications, since attitudes that lead straight to hell can be dismissed out of hand.

Yet the writer's job is not to disturb and then reassure his readers, but to challenge their understanding of themselves and others—which in relation to the philanderer means, I believe, that his fate must be left unresolved.

Moreover, what could any "resolution" signify except a facile opinion in lieu of comprehension? Many people would be glad to see the libertine end his life in poverty and solitude—but then isn't poverty and solitude the fate of a great many good and deserving people? "Here I think of all those who insist that Don Juan must be punished," wrote Camus in his essay *The Absurd Man*. "Not only in another life, but even in this one. I think of all those stories, legends, and jokes about the aging Don Juan. But Don Juan is ready. . . . The universe of which he has a glimpse contains *also* ridicule. He would find it normal to be punished. It's a rule of the game. And this is his greatness of spirit, that he has accepted all the rules of the game. But he knows that he is right and that there can be no question of punishment. A fate is not a punishment. That is his crime and one can understand why the men of God call for his punishment."

However, despite all righteous or malicious fantasies about people getting their "just deserts," a life's conclusion provides only an illusory connection with its history. The future neither justifies nor condemns the past; it merely follows it.

In *The Absurd Man*, Camus also says that Don Juan calls into question the significance we place on *time* as the measure of value. Does, for instance, the quality of love depend on how lasting it is? I don't intend to formulate here the ethical and philosophical questions I attempted to pose through the realities described in the novel, except to say that I didn't believe they could be considered seriously (in a new perspective, so to speak) without the overriding presence of physical love. For sex, next to death, gives us our deepest experience of the Absurd and is thus a major source of dislocation and confusion in our consciousness and our culture.

Sex is the bad news that we have no supernatural powers. At the moment when we most want to transcend ourselves, we run up against the confines of our humanity; in the act of love we cannot help discovering how far (or rather how near) we can extend beyond our skin. We like to think that we are shy of the body, but we are shy of the lesson that the soul exists in the flesh—in the flesh of exhaustible strength and inexhaustible weaknesses. Moreover, when we bare our body to another, we also bare our personality, at least to our own consciousness. Though a sadist may constrain himself to behave like a gentle lover, he cannot help knowing that he wants to draw blood. The sexual act burns away our self-image, at least for the moment, and confronts us with our self; it measures our capacities for feeling and perceiving, for affection, courage, hard work and joy—and exposes our pettiness, apathy, cowardice and selfishness. The popular Freudian notion is right in reverse:

it is not so much that sexual experience forms the character, *it is the character that determines the sexual experience.*

Thus our anxiety concerning sex is existential anxiety and (as I have tried to show through characters who have few moral or social inhibitions) it is inherent in the physical experience, regardless of our conscious attitudes. Whatever joy it offers is joy that grows out of dread. Which is also to say that the current myth of a "sexual revolution" is utter nonsense—as is the puritan's worry that people may now enjoy sex too much and too freely. There is no way for a man to free himself from the shock of self-awareness that is at the core of the erotic experience—unless it is by getting himself stone drunk.

The liberalization of law and public opinion and four-letter words in print have no power to deliver us from our existential terror and dream. If Sex is Fun now, it is fun like the Ten Commandments. An American psychiatrist has defined the present "sexual freedom" as the *New Puritanism*, in recognition of the fact that when we turn lovemaking into a compulsory sport, an etiquette of technique and a therapeutic prescription, we are simply finding new ways to minimize our involvement, to evade the testing of our being.

In literature, however, it is not so much the reflection of our own character that we wish to avoid (it is comparatively easy to dissociate oneself from fictional "undesirables") but the testing of our cherished beliefs and concepts. The realistic description of sexual behavior, impulses and experiences calls into question our most fundamental views about the nature of the human species and its place in the universe, the dualism of body and spirit (or intellect) which is still at the basis of Western culture. What is at stake in erotic literature is once again our notion of freedom. To what extent are we emancipated from our erotic instinct, and how much are we governed by it? The answer to this question is individual, not general, but one may conclude that whatever control we have over our bodies is more precious and less stable than we like to pretend. Few readers are upset enough to protest when they read about a fictional brute carried away by his impulses to torture and murder—and this is a welcome indication that the killer is an atypical character and that our personal impulses to cruelty and destruction are not so powerful as to give us cause for deep concern. The frequently hostile and even hysterical reaction to erotic realism, on the other hand, shows that it touches us "where it hurts." But again, I cannot possibly engage the reader with these questions by any sort of theoretical analysis: the calm forbearance with which readers tolerate every sort of *theory* about sex is a further confirmation that most people can think only their own thoughts and given ideas do not penetrate their mental defenses.

Realistic erotica might be defined as the fully conscious experience of the real thing. In life, the privacy of the shock makes it easier to ignore or explain away; what was disturbing may seem "accidental" and therefore irrelevant. But the printed text testifies to the universality of the experience and (as the reader is involved with his intellect and imagination rather than his whole being) reflection on its implications becomes almost inescapable. Which explains the apparent contradiction that many people who pursue sexual experience are embarrassed to read about it—that is, cannot bear to think about what it reveals. Today the main objection to sex in literature is that we know all about it.

As Brigid Brophy observed, sex is no longer immoral, it is boring; it isn't forbidden, just passé.

Still rarely does anyone have cause for discomfiture; there are very few truthful erotic novels. In literature, as in life, Eros is denied by desperate exaggerations—by pious tall tales, dirty jokes, and horror stories, born of dissatisfaction with the nature of our species.

St. Paul's ravings struck the most popular and enduring note of denial, denouncing sex as the Devil's instrument which brings out the animal in us. In this, St. Paul is the spiritual forefather of the Marquis de Sade and most pornographers—they all seem to view the bedroom as hell. Sartre's championing of Genet and Simone de Beauvoir's defense of Sade gave fashionable currency to the notion that pornographic nightmares expose the real depths of our being and that we manifest intellectual courage and advance the cause of enlightenment by facing up to such terrifying "truths" about ourselves. But the courage of Sade, Genet, or Burroughs reminds me of nothing so much as the ploy of the defense lawyer who exaggerates the prosecution's claims in order to make the charges so outrageous as to dwarf the actual offense. Their Don Juan goes to hell not only at the end of his life but every time he undresses. Whatever universal and therefore pertinent realities may emerge from his experience are canceled out by monstrous acts of cruelty and by an all-pervasive tone of disgust or hatred or *nostalgie de la boue* which makes them as irrelevant as the pleasures of a homicidal maniac.

This sort of thing will never lack readers, for in spite of the merry show, most people loathe sex.

There are evident reasons why we fear and detest what we pretend to enjoy so wholeheartedly. The agony of pretense and self-deception is one of them. Mainly, however, we hate sex, with the blind passion of our betrayed longings, for its broken promises of bliss: for its inability to unite us decisively with another human being, for the rarity of the right moment, for the unacknowledged disappointments and defeats we all suffer in bed, for the incessant reminders that nature is unjust and undemocratic in dispensing her gifts and that we are constantly losing even those attractions we possess as we grow older by the day. Yet we love sex too. It is the source of much of the pleasure we may have in life, and so there is the added curse of ambiguity—the unwilled fascination, the small reasons for great hopes. Not least, there is the grim envy of other people's luck, the dreadful suspicion that they are enjoying it more.

If that's how you feel, relax. You're a normal adult. Frustration, cowardice, envy and spite are part of the price we pay for not being gods. But such truths, however liberating, are unflattering, and human beings will stoop to anything to avoid knowing who they are. Thus the hatred of sex grows in a hothouse of lies. In the old days, this passion could find ideological justification and expression in puritan morality; now there is nothing left to hate with but pornography. People who are terrified of what might lurk in their souls and dare not look inward can never forgive mankind for their own cowardice, and turn on the world to seek grounds for detestation. That's what pornography is about—not sex, but fear of the self, and hatred.

Yet the sentimental poetic glorification of sexuality is equally false: whether we invest sex with evil or divine magic, we attribute to it a kind of spiritual reality that allows for the division of the soul and the body, introducing the supernatural into what is in fact the most compelling human evidence of its non-existence. Whether sex is viewed as a poison that depraves or an elixir that exalts us, it is mystified out of this world. Such pretensions only serve to create an attitude, to harden us against the immediacy of the experience, to predetermine our reactions to the revelations of intensified self-awareness. Both the worship and the profanation of Eros protect us from the loss of what we hold most sacred: the shield of our delusions.

"The Absurd Man," to quote Camus again, "multiplies what he cannot unify. In this way he discovers a new way of life which liberates him at least as much as it liberates those who come in contact with him. . . . All these deaths and all these rebirths make up for Don Juan the sheaf of his life. It is his way of giving and keeping alive." Which is to say, "Don Juan has chosen to be nothing." The value of such an attitude and such a life is almost beside the point; its psychological and social relevance, however, is of growing significance.

It seems to me that the philanderer's life demonstrates the basic paradox of personal freedom. The man who is not bound to anyone has no one bound to him. As he renounces his obligations to others, so he forfeits his claims upon them; his relationships being transitory, his alienation becomes permanent. Indeed, the libertine has always been as much pitied as envied, and one would suppose the duality of freedom and isolation to be one of the most widely understood human predicaments. Yet this understanding is rarely applied to *personal liberty*, the supreme goal of "progress," the end result of economic, technological and political changes that began with the Industrial

Revolution. The fact is, of course, that the increased opportunities for self-support, education, professional advancement according to ability, for birth control, divorce, migration (not to mention historical dislocations) have made millions lonelier as well as freer. Only a couple of generations ago most people died in the same town where they were born and had lifelong relationships with friends and foes alike, as well as with relatives and the sweethearts who grew up to marry them. Consequently, they could develop their capacity for lasting emotions, their ability to sustain basic relationships. Today few people live in the same community as their parents and relatives, childhood loves and friends, or indeed in any one place for very long; their associations change continually. What interested me in all this was the desolating sense of abruptness of modern life and the individual's emotional adaptation to the age of discontinuity: a way of feeling and perceiving that feeds on multiplying rather than deepening experience, and which I would call *episodic sensibility*. The libertine has become (from an extraneous "odd" character on the fringes of society) the representative hero of our time.

The question is, can our haste to succumb to joy, regardless of all other longings, reveal anything beyond the measure of our forlornness and despair?

A Place Where You Don't Feel Lonely

(EXCERPTS FROM A DIARY)

. . . I've been happy all day . . . there's no other reason for it but the place itself. It's so strange, it's evidently not like any of the places where I spend most of my life—I wouldn't be so affected by it if it were. During the whole day, I haven't been tempted once to close my eyes, to ignore what came into my field of vision—I haven't even seen a repulsive face, though this must have been an accident. I'm not used to being surrounded only by beautiful sights, that's why I must be feeling heady.

I'm writing this in my room in the Hôtel de Londres, on my big solid table facing the window, which faces the entrance court of the oldest royal palace in France, and the best. I can't see the whole château, of course (you can't do that except from the air)—I'm looking down at the Cour des Adieux and I can see the shadow of the great staircase,

(*229*)

two waves of stone leaping up the facade. It draws you to the building, then sends you back to take another look at the whole courtyard, the three wings with the merrily changing patterns of their mansard roofs. I was walking back and forth in the Cour des Adieux for an hour this morning, before I got around to the Carp Pond that edges up to the Fountain Court, which is yet another courtyard of another three-winged palace of an earlier period—or rather it's still the same palace but a different part of it. Fontainebleau is a smallish, self-contained building from any single angle—it dawned on me only after hours of walking how huge it really is. It is a masterpiece of architectural understatement.

The Carp Pond (with angry gold fish jumping into the air in their struggle for bread crumbs) encircles a royal love nest, a single octagonal room protected by the water. From the other side of the Pond I walk into the English Garden (there is nothing quite like it in England) where perfect statues of pretty women with exquisite small breasts, and pedestal busts with magnificent old faces stand among the trees and bushes, giving a dimension of human beauty to the woods. The magic of the mixture cannot be described, only experienced.

It is present even inside the palace. The rooms and corridors appear to exist only to provide space for the rendering of human figures in marble, stucco, and paint. Most of them are women and children—the babies are show-offs, thrusting out their chubby, cheerful bottoms from the doors, the walls and even the ceilings. And all this humanity frolics in a green shade, for the huge windows let in the gardens. I experienced today in a singular way the brotherhood of men and nature. . . . Diana with her dogs . . .

I started early today from Grenoble and planned to stop at Fontainebleau only for a couple of hours, intending to get back to London tonight, but I can't recall the sense of urgency which possessed me when I made my plans. Beauty is distracting. Which is the whole point—but it hadn't occurred to me before I watched the people strolling in the gardens as if they could never run out of time and I suddenly realized that it was years since I'd seen people quite so unhurried.

We're always in transit, worried about being late, oblivious of our route. The modern environment presses us inward, into a kind of mental hibernation—we try not to absorb the poison, not to see, not to respond. But the more efficient we become at ignoring everything which attacks our senses, the less we're able to sense our surroundings. We cease to look about in the world, we increasingly travel inside our skull, prey to unbroken chains of thought which turn into obsessions. Whatever filters through from the real world, we turn into further fantasy stuff.

So, on arrival, Fontainebleau is a jolt. I noticed in the François I Gallery, packed with the marvels of the Italian Renaissance (the first sight after one is let in through the visitors' entrance) that there was a lot of talk about hotel prices, restaurants, politics. But by the time we reached the Col de Cygne vestibule, everyone had forgotten about himself and was watching the statue of a small boy hugging a big swan, his dimpled fingers half-submerged in the plumage, while the swan strains forward and bends his long neck to drink the water.

. . . Obsession is the momentum of undistracted logic. So even when we forget about beauty, we suffer from her deadening absence—for beauty has the compelling power to distract us from ourselves, to rescue us from the worst loneliness of all, the isolation of fantasy life. . . .

20 *June*, FONTAINEBLEAU

. . . A couple of years ago, in Washington, I was so rude as to confess to a friend that I thought the White House would look cheap even beside the Bourbons' palace in Naples, on the Capodimonte, which never stored any real power. My friend dismissed my complaint. "You can't judge the White House from what you can see of it," he said impatiently. "Most of it is *underground*."

Here in Fontainebleau you're bound to feel kindly toward the ancient monarchs. In the Capodimonte or Versailles (Versailles stores the biggest collection of dukes and kings with mean, corrupt faces), it wasn't difficult to remember that the royal splendor was made from the sweat and blood of the poor. But modern rulers are spending more than royal fortunes on stockpiling missiles, sending junk into outer space and building underground labyrinths crammed with the gadgets of mad children, while half of mankind is hungry. The bad old king at least gave his subjects some notion of the joys he was robbing from them. He explored the possibilities of ideal living conditions. There is really no need for learned commissions and committees to ponder what people are missing. The research has been done, it's all here: buildings no higher than trees, wide rooms, high ceilings, big windows, works of art, ever present mementos of the past, and all this not far from birds, gardens and lakes.

I wish I could print a leaflet about this, a Fontainebleau manifesto, and distribute a few million copies around the suburbs and the slums—not that it would make the slightest difference. But then, nothing is impossible.

22 *June*, FONTAINEBLEAU

I was told that the rocks in the Temagami region of Northern Ontario had been there for 175,000,000,000 years, but they looked no more ancient than the small airplanes and motorboats, the gas stations and snack bars. Nature shows herself no older than her human frame and gives us no inkling of what went on before we were born, once we destroy the man-made signs.

At Fontainebleau I'm overwhelmed by the immensity of the past, though only a few walls date back even as far as the twelfth century, when it was first built as a hunting lodge for Louis VI.

The château, like all great works of art, has the live tension of contradictions. There's the dramatic blending of straight lines and curves—one could almost say that every straight line runs into a curve and they somehow balance, but just so . . . The building is alive because it has been growing through the centuries, as each king added a wing, a gallery or a pavilion. The style of each is rooted in its own period, but reflects all that preceded it, so time's passing is marked even though its continuity is unbroken. When you go through a doorway or up a staircase, you're walking into another century, yet the whole thing is still one piece. . . .

. . . I haven't felt so keenly for a long time how abandoned we are without the company of the dead. Perhaps we're obsessed with the future and find it difficult to relate to the present, because we're cut off from the past. Our sense of time is out of joint. There is no other way to explain the hysteria of everyday life and politics. The idea that it is better to have a nuclear war and annihilate mankind than to let the enemy "win" isn't trumpeted as much these days as it used to be, but the panic is still on. It's as if everything in history would happen *once and for all*.

Fontainebleau was Napoleon's favorite among all the royal palaces of France. Here he is more than the semifictional figure of monuments and history books—here one can sense that he was a living person—mementos of his daily life are everywhere. The love nest on the lake was built by Louis XIV, but it is called le Pavillon de l'Empereur and bears his proud N. I lingered on today in his bedroom in the château—it's a shock, how small a bed he needed, even though one knows he was a short man—the paintings tell tall stories. His bed is no bigger than a child's cot, though above it there is a king-size velvet canopy and the woodwork is swarming with his emblems—bees, N's, laurel wreaths and winged figures of Victory. In an antechamber, under a glass dome on a round table, rests the emperor's "small hat" which he wore while commanding his armies in the battles that won him most of Europe; and in the Map Room stands his great globe which he could spin around as he pleased, and to some consequence. Napoleon thought this château was the most fitting place from which to rule a continent: he called Fontainebleau "the house of the centuries, the true residence of kings." It was here, too, that he signed, incredulously, his abdication. Through my window I'm looking at the Cour des Adieux, with the leaping staircase. He walked down its steps on 20 April 1814 and said farewell to the still-faithful soldiers of his shrunken army, before he was taken away into exile. *Adieu, mes enfants!*

Today I cannot understand how people can talk about *decisive* victories or defeats. But I'm leaving tomorrow. We free ourselves from the past, and we live condemned to solitude in time.

The Fontainebleau Manifesto

WE RENOUNCE THE FUTURE.
WE DON'T CARE FOR VICTORIES.
WE DON'T WANT TO RULE OTHER MEN.
WE DON'T WANT TO CONQUER NATURE.
WE KNOW THAT DEATH DEFEATS US.
WE WANT TO RECONQUER THE PAST,
    LIVE FOR THE PRESENT,
    AND RULE ONLY OURSELVES.

OUR PRIDE IS THAT WE REMAIN SANE AND WILLING TO
    LOVE
DESPITE THE HORRORS OF THE WORLD,
BUT IT IS DIFFICULT.
WE CAN'T LIVE ON BREAD SOURED BY SQUALOR.
WE CAN'T BREATHE AIR POISONED BY DEATH
    FACTORIES.

ontainebleau Palace: Courtyard of Good-byes (GOURSAT from RAPHO GUILLUMETTE)

WE DON'T NEED MISSILES, CARS, COMPUTERS, ELECTRIC
    TOOTHBRUSHES.
WE CAN DO WITHOUT ALL THE JUNK GREAT KINGS
    COULD DO WITHOUT,
BUT WE CANNOT LIVE WITHOUT AIR, THE FORESTS, THE
    FIELDS AND THE RIVERS,
GREAT SQUARES AND GARDENS AND YES, OUR
    PALACES.
IT IS A LIE THAT THE WORLD CANNOT AFFORD SPLEN-
    DOR FOR EVERYONE—
WE RENOUNCE REAL-ESTATE VALUES.

WE CANNOT LIVE WITHOUT BEAUTY;
MANY OF US SEEK IT IN DRUGS
    AND ALCOHOL AND HATE.
WE TRY NOT TO SUCCUMB TO SUBSTITUTES
BUT IT IS DIFFICULT.
THE WORLD NEEDS A ROYAL REVOLUTION
SO THAT ALL MEN MAY LIVE LIKE KINGS.

THANKS AND ACKNOWLEDGMENTS

Michael Ratcliffe, literary editor of *The Times,* knew before I did that I must write about Stendhal, and his insistence that I should do so was responsible not only for "One of the Very Few" but also for my persevering with the book, at a time when I was ready to give it up.

I originally argued some of the ideas in this book in *The Times, The Spectator, Archives Diplomatiques et Consulaires,* and *The Village Voice.*

Acknowledgment is due to the authors and publishers of the following works which are quoted in *The Rules of Chaos.*

The Confessions of Nat Turner by William Styron, published by Random House, Inc. *Catch-22* by Joseph Heller, published by Simon & Schuster, Inc. The poem "Exit Lines" from *The Absolute Smile* by George Jonas, published by the House of Anansi, Toronto. *American Negro Slave Revolts* by Herbert Aptheker, published by International Publishers Co., Inc. *Division Street: America* by Studs Terkel, published by Pantheon Books, Inc. *War and Peace* by Leo Tolstoy, translated by Rosemary Edmonds and published by Penguin Books. Other translations are the author's own.